To Dad on your 80th
Birthday,
Jean+Ron
xxx
xxx

BOBBY ROBSON

Newcastle

MY KIND OF TOON

HODDER &
STOUGHTON

First published in Great Britain in 2008 by Hodder & Stoughton
An Hachette Livre UK company

I

Copyright © Bobby Robson 2008

The right of Bobby Robson to be identified as the Author of the Work
has been asserted by him in accordance with the Copyright, Designs and
Patents Act 1988.

A CIP catalogue record for this title is available from the British Library

ISBN 978 0 340 97783 5

Typeset in Scala and Stone Sans

Printed and bound by Mohn Media in Germany

Hodder & Stoughton policy is to use papers that are natural, renewable and
recyclable products and made from wood grown in sustainable forests.
The logging and manufacturing processes are expected to conform to the
environmental regulations of the country of origin.

Hodder & Stoughton Ltd
338 Euston Road
London NW1 3BH

To my dear wife Elsie,
my family and the wonderful people
of the North East

CONTENTS

Acknowledgements   9

Introduction   10

1   GOING TO THE MATCH   16

2   SATURDAY NIGHT   32

3   SUNDAYS   50

4   THE WORKING WEEK   68

5   LEISURE TIME   100

6   THE HEART OF THE CITY   122

7   HEARTBEAT OF THE CITY   150

8   FURTHER AFIELD   186

9   NEWCASTLE HEROES   218

    Epilogue   244

ACKNOWLEDGEMENTS

Although I was born and bred in the North East, the process of assembling this book has shown me that you're never too old to learn, even about people and places you consider familiar. By its very nature, this is a personal selection of memories, photographs and anecdotes rather than a factual record, so I hope that any omissions will be indulged. By the same token, while Newcastle is in the title of the book and both the city and its football club feature prominently, my intention is not to exclude; I'm the product of a region rather than of a specific place in it and my affections spread both north and south of the Tyne.

I could not have undertaken a project such as this without the help of many people. Roddy Bloomfield at Hodder and Stoughton, who commissioned the book, is like the best sort of football manager – inspirational, intuitive and always on hand to dish out encouragement. Roddy wears his expertise lightly, but he is pre-eminent in his field and producing the words to justify his limitless faith is something I've strived for.

I must pay a special tribute to Gabrielle Allen, who has poured time, energy and enthusiasm into unearthing the emotive photographs that grace the following pages. Her research has captured brilliantly the beauty and essence of my home. Gabrielle's professionalism and dedication is matched by that of Marion Paull, copy editor supreme. As ever, Judith Horey, my personal secretary and a Newcastle girl, has been wonderful, checking details, ferrying me to meetings and offering tireless support.

I chose George Caulkin to turn my thoughts into words because I knew precisely what I'd get – a first-rate journalistic talent, application and, as a fellow alumni of Langley Park infants school, someone who shares my passion for the area. What I didn't know is that George would donate his fee to my charitable foundation. As most people will recognise, I'm rarely left speechless, but his remarkable gesture certainly did the trick. My warm thanks to him.

Without the love, sustenance and patience of my dear family, particularly in recent times, I would be nothing. This is their history, their heritage, as much as mine. The North East, of course, is responsible for the most important event of my life – meeting Elsie, my stunning, delightful wife, my rock and my muse.

INTRODUCTION

I WAS BORN into a black-and-white world. Some of my earliest, most treasured memories are set in monochrome. Every morning my father, who was a proud colliery man for fifty-one years, would leave our home in Langley Park, Co. Durham white as a sheet and return each evening black, covered from head to hobnail boots in coal dust. For an ardent supporter of Newcastle United, as my dad was and I would quickly become, the colour scheme was appropriate.

The murky gloom of the pit, the blinding gleam of the floodlights – they are the dominant shades of my life. As someone who has been privileged enough to win at Wembley, to play for and manage my country, to work in Holland, Portugal and Spain, I've seen vivid sights and been surrounded by excitement, but black and white is where it began and black and white I've always been. Even when I was managing Barcelona, that marvellous maelstrom of a football club, I'd reach the haven of the dressing-room and ask someone to find out 'how Newcastle have got on', a query that most exiled Geordies will find familiar.

Newcastle the club and Newcastle the city surge through my blood. All this time later, I can still hear my father telling me about the FA Cup final in 1932, which he'd attended the year before I was born, when United beat Arsenal 2–1. He'd won a ticket in a competition run by the *Evening Chronicle*.

LEFT: Back to where it all began. After a long career in football, I'm a fan again now. Here I am at St James' Park, watching my beloved Newcastle United, the team I supported as a boy and went on to manage. Down in the dug-out or patrolling the touchline, there was barely any wind, but I've found out just how cold it can be when you're elevated in the stands, and I'm usually glad of the scarf my son, Paul, gave me for Christmas. The hat's useful, too, but there's still nothing like a home victory to warm me up.

OVERLEAF: This was one of the proudest moments of my life. The Robson clan pose with the lord mayor and lady mayoress on the day I was made an honorary Freeman of Newcastle upon Tyne. Alan Shearer, another Freeman, attended the ceremony. I told the audience about my black-and-white heritage, how my father went down the pit white and came home black. Doesn't my wife look lovely, by the way!

Albert Stubbins was my first idol, but there would be many others. I remember seeing Len Shackleton's first game for the club, when he scored six goals against Newport County, and the names of those players who won such a firm place in my affections in those early years still roll off the tongue – Henry Clifton, George Hair, Richard Burke, little Ernie Taylor, Tommy Walker, Norman Dodgin, Frank Brennan, Charlie Crowe, Tom Swinburne, Jackie Milburn, of course, the Robledo brothers. I can recall Bobby Mitchell ripping Alf Ramsey apart when the future England manager was a studious, if slow, full back and Bobby had this step-over trick with his left foot. Legends, all of them.

Each generation has its own legendary figures – Malcolm Macdonald, Kevin Keegan, Paul Gascoigne, Chris Waddle, Peter Beardsley and Alan Shearer, to name but a small selection, have all passed into Geordie folklore – but what unites United is loyalty to the club and a fierce devotion. Supporters everywhere believe, quite rightly, that their own favourite club is special, but it is my firm contention that Newcastle has a history, culture and location that make it wonderfully, beguilingly different. It is a single-club city, with a stadium at its heart, sitting flush among some architectural jewels, in a region where a football result, good or bad, can affect productivity at work and shape the mood of a week.

Two trams rattle along Neville Street in front of Central Station in 1946, one *en route* to Newton Road and the other to Scotswood. They were a familiar sight when I made my early trips to the city to cheer on United. Are northerners more impervious to the cold? These days it's shirt sleeves and bare legs in the Bigg Market; back then it was the open-topped upper deck!

Supporters mingle outside the famous Strawberry pub before a pre-season friendly in 2004 – my last summer as Newcastle manager. Losing my job, so soon after we'd finished fifth in the League, was a huge personal blow and one I didn't deserve. Some members of my family felt more hurt than I did, but I never lost my love for the club. You can change much in life, but not the colour of your blood.

RIGHT: Inside the Strawberry, in the shadow of the Gallowgate End, the pre-match ritual of a pint and amateur punditry takes place under the gaze of the black-and-white heroes adorning the walls. I went there once or twice. If truth be told, Newcastle has 52,000 managers, not one. Everyone has an opinion, a story, some gossip. It makes for an exhilarating atmosphere.

ABOVE: Supporters waiting outside the stadium in 1938. Dad, Ron and I would try to be at the ground first. There was a lady we used to see every fortnight, a mad-keen fan like ourselves, and our aim was to beat her to the front of the queue. My dad always had a chat with her.

RIGHT: The walk to the match would be filled with hope and possibly some trepidation. Putting smiles on people's faces later became my task. This scene is very different from the one that featured in my childhood. We hung about outside the gates and then ran up the hill when they opened, so we would be first to pay our money and through the turnstiles. We'd perch in the front row of the unreserved seats, waiting impatiently for the spectacle to begin.

PREVIOUS SPREAD: From whichever direction you approach Newcastle, St James' Park is visible. It dominates the landscape, which is distinctly fitting for such a football-centric place. It's less a stadium than a cathedral, made for Saturday worship. Barcelona's Nou Camp and the Bernebeu in Madrid might be bigger grounds, but you don't really notice them until you're right on top of them. St James' Park is different – like a beacon, like the Eddystone Lighthouse. It stands up above the town and looks over it. The place brings its own pressure, but I thrived on it.

of club that swallows up hard work. In my final year there, I couldn't spare a single day off for a game of golf because there was always something pulling me to the club, so to make it work, you have to be a campaigner and someone who knows the track.

The obvious exception to that blueprint is Kevin Keegan, whose appointment as manager the first time around came as a bolt from the blue, when he'd been away from the game for so long, enjoying the Spanish sun and working on his golf handicap. What he did was phenomenal, but he captures a special resonance in the Geordie psyche. Having been a little messiah of a player, he came back at a moment when the club had passed into new ownership and, aside from a desperate league position, was ready for lift-off, and he carried everyone with him by virtue of his enthusiasm, effervescence and knowledge of the area. Considering he didn't have the experience that Arsene Wenger, Sir Alex Ferguson, Brian Clough, Jock Stein or Bill Shankly had, his achievement was extraordinary. On the day Kevin returned for a second stint in charge, in January 2008, and his third spell at the club, I was in the city centre and I couldn't believe the emotion I witnessed. His presence generated hysteria, absolute hysteria. I've never known one man have such an effect on a club in a matter of a few hours, and I saw the queue for tickets snake around the stadium and felt the tremors of excitement. Yes, it was a surprise appointment, but it was also a popular one and worth a try because he's such a charismatic, uplifting figure and Newcastle were in the doldrums. The people at the club must have known they had to provide a boost to everyone, and if they were asking themselves who was the one guy who, in terms of exhilaration and pleasure, could restore things to what they were, they picked the right candidate. As a player and manager, Kevin has built a career on defying logic and perceived wisdom. Good luck to him.

Logic has seldom been the Newcastle way, though – a black-and-white city where little is black and white, where everyone has an opinion, a story to tell, gossip to impart and a team to pick, where the volume is set permanently on loud and where passions soar. Football has changed beyond recognition since I was being hypnotised by Albert Stubbins and so has the arena he graced, but I'd still defy anyone to sit in St James' Park on a crisp winter afternoon, the breath misting in front of their face, and hear the first few lusty bars of the 'Blaydon Races' tumble from the stands, grow and spread around the stadium, and not feel elated or a stirring in their soul. No surprise there. The harmonics may be less than pitch-perfect, but the power is of a cathedral choir.

RIGHT: Liverpool is famous for its 'This is Anfield' sign, Newcastle has 'Howay the Lads'. You can almost hear the shouts of encouragement from the dressing-room, the roar of the crowd. When I was appointed manager, this was just a grubby corridor with plain walls that would quickly get dirty. We wanted the view to be uplifting for our own players and intimidating to the opposition.

OVERLEAF: Marvellous monochrome. Newcastle fans come in all shapes and sizes, but the twin colours prevail. They say that not everything in black and white makes sense and the club can make your head swim, but I hope they never change the purity of the stripes. The scarf-twirling is a more recent innovation, but the effect is dazzling.

2
SATURDAY NIGHT

AS A FORMER manager of Newcastle United, I need no schooling in the allure provided by the city's nightspots and watering holes. In those days, a siren's peril lurked on my doorstep – not for me, I hasten to add. I steered clear of the famous Bigg Market and the lively quayside, knowing that as a familiar face attached to a keenly supported club, there was a danger of being mobbed. It was a far safer bet to go straight home to Elsie! But the reasons for my trepidation were an attraction to others. For young, athletic men with a few pounds to spend, the temptations were obvious.

The rhythms of the week on Tyneside are seductive and deeply engrained. I'm sure that much of it is connected to the heavy industry that once powered the city. The work was arduous, physically demanding, so when the weekend rolled up, the opportunity for Newcastle people to exhale, blow out their cheeks and lose themselves a little bit was embraced with abandon. Football's role in the process was elemental. Frustrations were released, passion was fierce. Win, lose or draw, supporters would congregate afterwards to discuss the merits or the flaws of what they'd witnessed, the glory and the injustices, over a pint or two in the countless pubs dotted around the area. The world turns and things change, but not that. Never that.

I have no problem with the bright lights and pulsating music that emanate from the city on Friday and Saturday nights. Quite the opposite. As you can see from the squadrons of stag and hen parties that are disgorged from the railway station and weave through the streets, Newcastle has transformed itself into a party capital, and is a world-class venue for celebration. Leisure has become an industry in itself, making the most of a quality we could already boast about – graft to the utmost and then let your hair down – with a wide variety of old-fashioned pubs, trendy modern bars and nightclubs.

Even in my line of work, the development of the city was of notable benefit, something away from football that you could use judiciously to attract a player. Joining a new club is not just about the name on the shirt, the trophies in the cabinet, the thickness of the wage-packet, or the reputation of the manager. Most players want to better themselves, but there are practicalities to consider, including where your family may want to live.

Night in the city. Come rain or shine, Newcastle is rarely less than animated when the weekend approaches. This looks like the calm before, or after, the storm.

ABOVE: Members of the working-men's club could usually be found deep in discussion, and the latest events at St James' Park would almost certainly be on the agenda. The club played a vital role in the social life of our village, whether as a place for relaxation away from the pit or through organising outings. My dad was a Methodist and a teetotaller, but he would go there every week to play dominoes and cards.

RIGHT: Brown ale in hand, a member of the bar staff patrols the aisles at the Byker and St Peter's Working Men's Social Club on a Saturday night in 1973. Never much of a drinker, I avoided Newcastle at night when I returned as manager. Even when I worked with England I could walk down the street without being noticed, but in Barcelona and Newcastle, where football is king, I'd be recognised instantly.

Girls dance to a live band at Byker and St Peter's. Newcastle has always been a great place for letting your hair down after a long week, but I think this singer may have taken it a step too far! Thankfully, fashion is temporary, but the city's reputation as a party destination holds firm.

Jazz fans sit in rapt attention at
the Club Martinique in 1955.
Newcastle is still renowned for
its music venues.

Local facilities, the shops, the atmosphere around you also have to be taken into account. A thriving, bouncing city in thrall to its team was a huge asset to United, although it came with the significant caveat that the players understood their responsibilities and knew how to behave.

There were two aspects to the rules I set out. Ahead of a Saturday game, I didn't want the lads over-exerting themselves or going anywhere from Wednesday onwards. They were to steer well clear of clubs, pubs, bars and parties. But after playing at St James', it was different. I couldn't tell them not to go out, because they were fit, good-looking, had a bit of money and wanted a social life. You can't expect them to be monks. So what I used to say to them was, 'Relax, wind down, enjoy yourselves, but look, you don't have to be out until three or four in the morning. That'll just get you into trouble. Remember that for your job you have to be fit and in great condition. You're professional sportsmen.'

A Newcastle dance hall in 1954. My eldest brother Tom was the great dancer of the family. He and his wife Marion competed in the local area and would catch the bus to the Oxford Galleries in Newcastle for the tea-dance most Saturdays. A big orchestra was one of the attractions.

I liked my players to be married, because then there would be some sort of control or grounding from their wives, but there were a lot of single boys at Newcastle. I never had trouble from most of them. If I found out that anybody had been carousing within seventy-two hours of a game, they'd be whacked. 'Know who you are and what you represent,' I'd tell them, 'because people will damn well know who you are. Behave yourselves. If you get into bother, you'll be on the front pages, not the back, and we won't be able to save you, so just don't give us problems. Don't hit the waiter.' We laid that down every single week. Even so, the club would still put out scouts and the odd little tale would be relayed back to me. I knew that the players would be besieged by the public, because footballers in Newcastle are like matadors in Spain – sporting gods.

By and large, they behaved. Alan Shearer, Warren Barton and Gary Speed never went off the rails, but I understood that one or two of the players hadn't been brought up in the same way and were drawn to the nightlife. As I say, I didn't mind that, but stay out until the early hours and they were going to get talked about. I drummed into them that they had to act responsibly, because by the time Monday morning rolled around, they had to be down at the training ground, on the track and ready for duty. They weren't sitting at a desk, pushing a pen around. But just as I didn't socialise with my squad, I couldn't insulate them from their surroundings for twenty-four hours of every day. Embracing responsibility is part of maturing. Some people had to learn from their mistakes.

I've heard about the enticements Tyneside has to offer, but only seen them from a distance. I've eaten in restaurants on the quayside – I used to have an office down there – and popped into the Pitcher and Piano during the comparative lull of lunchtime. I once drove through the quayside at night and couldn't believe what I saw – troops of young women, ten or fifteen in a group, sporting short sleeves and the skimpiest clothes I'd ever seen in my life. 'My God, look at that,' I thought. I locked the car doors and sailed through! But it's part of a city that is growing up. If the place was dull, why would anybody come here? It isn't and they do. In droves.

I was too young to experience Newcastle at night when, still a raw teenager, I left Langley Park. In any case, I didn't have the money, or a car. My parents didn't allow alcohol or cigarettes to be consumed in the house and, when I played, there was little or no pub culture. Recreational drinking really began to be a feature of football during my spell in management. I was aware of it when I took over at Ipswich Town. You have to remember that until 1961, the maximum wage for footballers was just

£20 per week, so nobody could afford to sit around in pubs, drinking their livelihoods away. By the 1970s, society was changing. The pressure grew on players, the rewards on offer multiplied and they would seek release in lager and champagne.

Don Howe, my coach with England, would lambast them. 'I don't understand you lot,' he would say. 'You punish your bodies twice on a Saturday. You punish it by playing a rugged game and then at night you go out and punish it again with alcohol, knowing that you'll be bloody hopeless in training afterwards. You can't recover in twenty-four hours.' And it did have an impact. Players would often be difficult to train due to the after-effects of alcohol, even at a time when we were all learning more about nutrition and the benefits of refuelling properly.

In recent times, some managers have developed a fascination for wine, the grape varieties and the different vintages. I've seen Sir Alex Ferguson's wine cellar and it's a big deal. The great man would never struggle to open up his own off-licence. He knows his stuff, does Alex, but as I'm sure his Manchester United players would testify, he also knows that sport and over-indulgence are uneasy companions.

I never drank very much, so meeting people in pubs was never part of my scene. The fleeting moments away from the stresses of the game were more about emptying my brain of training-ground routines, scouting reports and tactics, rather than making it addled or woozy. Elsie and I had three children, so spending time with my young family was a priority. I played golf when I could, I read a bit more and television became more pleasurable. Before my latest illness and disability, I used to love gardening. I could do it without thinking, which was precisely the pleasure it afforded me, immersing myself in physical activity – picking out weeds, cutting the grass, trimming the hedges, edging, making things neat and tidy. I'm a bit fastidious when it comes to things like that. I couldn't leave a bit of paper lying around. I hate mess. And a messy mind was no use in my job. People think management must be easy, but running a football club at the highest level is the most difficult task in sport. It's amazing. You're trying to get consistent results, judge players, scout for new ones, prepare for games, watch opponents, organise training. At Ipswich, I dealt with transfers and negotiated contracts. I even bought the toilet rolls! And when the board of directors were split, it was up to me to cast the deciding vote over whether we built a new stand or not, a decision that would cost the club millions of pounds. No, a thick head and muddled thinking would not have been enjoyable.

As someone once said, you don't have to drink to enjoy yourself. My dad was a teetotaller, but once a week he'd go to the working-men's club in Langley Park to try his hand at dominoes, bridge and whist. He was a very good card player. Social clubs played a major part in people's lives in working communities, providing colleagues with the chance to relax in each other's company. It was a communal centre and very popular. When Tom, my eldest brother, reached the ripe old age of sixteen, Dad put his name down in the hope that, by eighteen, he would be eligible for membership. The waiting list was that long. The whole village went to the club. Ours had three snooker tables, a card room and a drinking room. Snooker was a big thing. Sometimes people would play skittles on the baize, knocking pins into pockets or avoiding them.

I might not have seen Newcastle in full swing, but Tom did. He started work down the mine the day after the Second World War was declared. His hobby was dancing, at the same local Parochial Hall where later I met Elsie, and he and his wife, Marion, used to dance in competitions. When the Americans came to this country, they brought dance bands with them and Tom and Marion would follow them about to places such as Gilesgate in Durham. Sometimes they would have to walk home to Langley Park. I used to love watching them practise. They had such poise and grace, moving in an upright stance. They were dazzling.

Their recreation took them to the Oxford Galleries in Newcastle, which Tom told me was a marvellous venue, with a big old-fashioned orchestra to dance to, and usually packed out. They would perform the Viennese Waltz, the foxtrot and quickstep, the kind of routine you would see on *Come Dancing*. Saturday-afternoon tea-dances were their regular engagement, because transport was restricted and they had to make sure they were in good time to catch the bus home from there. There were only three cars in our village then and two of them – one an old Lanchester – belonged to the doctor.

Sadly, the tea-dances are no more, but rather like much of Newcastle, the Oxford has been reinvented. The name has changed, more than once I'm told, but the building still stands and the function remains the same. Young people still flock there to strut their stuff.

OVERLEAF: Tyneside may be black and white, but when the sun goes down, the quayside is awash with colour and presents a skyline to rival any city's. Newcastle offers entertainment galore. Eat, drink and be merry.

ABOVE: Drinkers savouring a cosy tipple at the Crown Posada on Dean Street. A narrow bar with stained-glass windows and an old record player, the pub is an institution in Newcastle and regularly packed.

RIGHT: One of the oldest buildings in Newcastle, the Cooperage pub is reputed to be haunted. From drinking dens to sophisticated night spots, people with a thirst to quench do not lack options.

OVERLEAF: Newcastle has somewhere to suit every taste and here the Apartment bar is crammed with revellers on its grand opening in 2003. A rich and varied nightlife was an attraction when it came to signing players at Newcastle, but I had to warn them to respect their club and themselves. Dedicated athletes practise moderation.

3

SUNDAYS

SQUIRMING in my best clothes – or best hand-me-downs, anyway – still gleaming from my weekly bath two nights earlier, every Sunday morning would find the young Bobby Robson traipsing to the Methodist chapel in Langley Park with my family. I've never been a particularly religious person, but my parents were, so choice didn't come into it – it was chapel and Sunday school for me, morning and afternoon. Dredging back through the decades, the hymns we sang still rise to my lips: 'The king of love my shepherd is, whose goodness faileth never.' Sunday dinner was always a pleasure. We had Yorkshire puddings first, followed by beef – if we were lucky – and vegetables, then apple crumble, or something like that, for pudding. Mum was a terrific cook, using the oven next to the fire, always wearing her trusty pinny.

Later on in life, my father moved to the Church of England and became passionate about that, giving up his time and making efforts for local charitable causes. Elsie, my wonderful wife, has always been a good Catholic girl. She's still a regular worshipper – twice a week – and it's strange to think now that there was an element of tension between the different Christian faiths in our village. That was never part of my mentality. For me, church means the cool, tranquil majesty of Durham Cathedral, which always enthrals me. It means the inspiring architecture I would pass on my way to work at Newcastle – the Cathedral Church of St Nicholas with the lantern spire, which once guided shipping on the Tyne, the Roman Catholic Cathedral of St Mary's, close to the Central Station, and St Andrews Church, said to be the oldest in the city, nestling on Gallowgate, around the corner from the stadium.

After Sunday duty came pleasure. Before St James' Park became a regular destination, the highlight of my week followed chapel, when we'd set off up the New Road out of the village, away from the mine and into the fresh air, towards Witton Gilbert, where my grandmother lived. We'd have our finery on, and my dad would be sporting his dut, a kind of bowler hat. Ever the budding footballer, I'd kick all the loose stones I came across, earning frequent clips around the ear and shouts of, 'Don't do that!' As well as being a miner and general handyman, my father was also a cobbler. He would mend all of our old shoes. I can still see him with his mouth full of

What an extraordinary picture. Could anything better sum up north-east life as it once was? Children play football in Wallsend while over the street wall, in the dockyard beyond, the Shell tanker *Narica* is being built. Launched in 1967 from the Swan Hunter shipyard, it weighed more than 115,000 tonnes. Kids would kick a ball about anywhere. Wherever there was a spare patch of ground, there'd be a match going on. My youthful games took place in the midst of mine workings.

tacks, working with the iron foot he'd shape the shoe or boot around, cutting and trimming the leather with a sharp knife. No wonder he'd get upset when I attempted to emulate Albert Stubbins. But it wouldn't stop him splashing out on a twopenny cornet each for my brothers and me as we wended our way home. When we got there, Dad would run a clothes brush over his dut and put it away until the following Sunday.

For us, and for thousands of families across the region, special Sunday outings, or rare free time, would mean the North Sea, and the coast, more often than not, meant Whitley Bay, or sometimes South Shields. Given our lack of a car, a luxury we couldn't afford, travelling wasn't an easy proposition. We'd catch the bus to Newcastle and then take the train, but the journey merely added to the bubbling anticipation of the sights and sounds that awaited us – the busy white beaches and roiling waves, the gleaming white dome of the Spanish City and the funfair inside. We didn't have much money to mess around with, but I remember playing the penny-in-the-slot machines. Local organisations, Sunday school, the working-men's club or the temperance society would organise village trips.

A stained-glass window at St Martin's, Byker. During my early years I'd have to attend chapel and Sunday school in Langley Park, but I've never been a deeply religious person. Elsie is a practising Catholic. Strange as it may seem these days, there was tension between the different Christian denominations in Langley Park when I was growing up.

This statue of Cardinal Basil Hume, which stands outside the Roman Catholic St Mary's Cathedral, was unveiled by the Queen in 2002. It's a good likeness. The former Archbishop of Westminster was a Newcastle boy. My career has brought me into contact with many famous people, including Princess Diana – who was beautiful, stunning – and Prime Ministers Heath, Wilson, Callaghan, Thatcher, Blair and Brown.

ABOVE: I'm sure the Giant Wheel that features in this modern photo of the Hoppings offers fine views over Tyneside, but I'll always associate Newcastle with a roller-coaster. That's what it felt like to manage the club. There was never a dull moment.

RIGHT: The morning after the night before … people still throng to Newcastle's quayside for the Sunday market, which has been in existence since at least the 1700s. Once the domain of fairground attractions and racing tipsters, it now attracts shoppers on the hunt for bargains or hangover cures. It's a beautiful setting.

ABOVE: The Town Moor, a vast, peaceful oasis on the edge of the city, is where Freemen have grazing rights. As my title is an honorary one, apparently that benefit doesn't stretch to me – I suppose it's fortunate that I don't own any cattle. What a contrast there is between the greenery in the foreground and the busy city behind.

RIGHT: Newcastle is blessed with ample green spaces and this is a fine one. Leafy Jesmond Dene is a beautiful spot for young families to roam and for shady walks along the banks of the Ouseburn. Two of the city's best restaurants are here, too.

We'd sit on the crowded beach – Whitley Bay was the Scottish equivalent of Blackpool and for a fortnight each year, the Scots would swarm there – muck about, walk the prom, indulge in bare-foot kickabouts. There were rows upon rows of tents, where you could find shelter and the more adventurous would get changed into bathing costumes beneath their towels. Even in the height of summer, the sea was seldom friendly. Flinty blue, the water was also a deep freeze, but while some lads would walk in step by perishing step, I used to get it over with and throw myself in. I've always been impulsive. The cold was numbing, but we'd swim while we could tolerate it before racing up the beach to the warmth of the sun and scalding tea poured from a flask. Eating in restaurants was beyond our means, so it would be sandwiches and lemonade, all carried by my dad. Sometimes we must have been treated to a more substantial meal, because I remember the salty, sandy, vinegar tang of fish and chips, eaten from newspaper.

There might be a stroll to the imposing St Mary's Lighthouse, scouring rock-pools beneath it for starfish, or south to Cullercoats and the priory at Tynemouth, which has always been a pretty, genteel sort of place, with its weekend flea and antique markets in the restored Victorian station. It was a family affair then and still is, because Andrew, one of my sons, now lives in Tynemouth. As the years went on, we'd sometimes spend our holidays in Blackpool, but Mrs Foreshaw's guest house in Whitley Bay was the usual venue. I don't remember my parents having any kind of holiday until after the war, but that was where we went for three or four years. The Foreshaws were Sacriston people. Treasured days.

At seventeen, my world changed. I moved to London to play for Fulham and suddenly I had to get used to city living. I considered myself an adult. I had no parents to chaperone me around, so I had to stand on my own feet, live by my own standards, make my own decisions and work my way through life. For the first few months, I carried on my apprenticeship as an electrician, working for a living for a company that had part of the lighting contract for the Festival of Great Britain site. My football suffered. I was getting up early, returning home at six, training on Tuesday and Thursday nights and then playing for the reserves on Saturdays.

In those manic days, my Sundays were simply about recovery. I'd walk in the park, rest up, read a bit, eat with my landlord and landlady. I was on my own because Tom Wilson, the buddy I shared digs with, came from Southampton and would go home to see his girlfriend. At the rate I was going, I realised that I wasn't going to make the grade.

This is Central Station in 1936. On special Sunday outings, we'd catch the train from here to Whitley Bay. The call of the North Sea was strong, and the closer we got to the coast, the more excited I became. Training would eventually mean something different to me.

Tynemouth railway station in the 1950s, when I first became familiar with it. Originally opened in 1882, it is used by the Metro service now and its ornate canopy and footbridge make it an impressive site. Every weekend it hosts flea and antiques markets.

ABOVE: At the seaside with my brothers Ron (*left*) and Phil (*right*). Ron was the brainy one. He became secretary to the local colliery manager. Philip went on to become a master builder. He built my home for me in Ipswich. I called it Durham House.

RIGHT: Not the Copacabana or Bondi Beach, but Costa del Tynemouth. Can you believe how crowded it was? Look at the changing huts, the number of people swimming. But this is what people did for their holidays in 1957. When I was still a boy, the number of cars in our village could be counted on one hand and cheap air travel to places such as Spain or Greece was unthinkable. This was taken in the year I won my first England cap, against France.

The time came when I had to tell my dad that I hadn't taken the monumental step of leaving home to become an electrician. I could have stayed at home to do that. I packed in my job, began full-time training and really enjoyed being a professional footballer.

It wasn't until I headed back north, almost fifty years later, to take the reins at my beloved Newcastle United, that I fully began to appreciate the joys that surround us. Through cheap air travel, the mysteries of the planet have been opened up for mass consumption, but one of my great pleasures has been discovering the delights that most Novocastrians take for granted. Cars are plentiful now, so the beauty of Bamburgh, the unspoilt wilds of the coastline and the empty splendour of the Northumberland countryside, once far beyond my reach, are all within easy driving distance for day-trips. In those hectic, restless months when United dominated my thoughts and deeds, breathing space was non-existent and weekends reserved for matches or warm-downs, but since leaving the job, I've expanded my horizons. I've been to Seahouses and Hexham, seen Hadrian's Wall and retraced my childhood steps to the fish quay at North Shields.

To a little boy fresh from the village, Newcastle felt like a magical but daunting place, full of busy people and crammed shopping streets, looming buildings and fans swarming to and from St James' Park. It would have seemed like heresy to me then, but there are plenty of other parks, too. Newcastle is a city of green spaces, from Leazes Park, the first to be established on Tyneside for the purposes of general relaxation, to serene Jesmond Dene, a haven for courting couples and young families, with its woodland paths and pets' corner. Then there is the biggest of them all, the Town Moor, with Exhibition Park and its boating lake, military museum and games facilities at the south-eastern corner, and a mammoth expanse of open land beyond. Once used for mining and agriculture, the Moor is Newcastle's lungs. How many other cities can offer such a stunning contrast as grazing cattle and the urban jungle in a single vista?

There are few limitations on Sundays now. Shoppers throng to the Metro Centre or Northumberland Street, bargains can be had at the quayside market, and the banks of the Tyne are perfect for strolling or cycling. Museums and cinemas, galleries and music venues, fine restaurants and pubs are open for business – Newcastle and its surroundings have been transformed into a genuine leisure hub and tourist destination.

Sunday is a day for families, for long lunches and get-togethers, for heated dissections of the previous afternoon's match. As traditions have

With trousers rolled up and skirt hitched high, a couple brave the chill at Whitley Bay in 1948. What a great picture! It took some nerve to dip your toes into that icy water, I can tell you.

weakened and the demands of television have multiplied, it is often a day for football itself. But most of all, it is a day for people; north-east people are the best of them. I think back to my dad, that Geordie coal miner, with a sense of wonder – how much enthusiasm must you have in your body to do that job for as long as he did? We're a hard-working folk, decent, honest, straight, reliable, who like a good laugh and a story or two. We're proud of where we're from and the accents that prove it. We don't try to hide it. In all the years I was abroad, I met hundreds of Geordies and no matter how long they'd been away from home or how far they'd travelled, they stayed true to their roots. When I returned, I adjusted straightaway. I was home.

We deal well with shared adversity. We always have. Some of my earliest, dimmest memories are of the Second World War. It started when I was six. I remember the black-outs, when every window in our modest house had to be sealed so the German aircraft would have no chinks of light to guide them. I can still hear the shrill tone of the air-raid sirens warning of approaching bombers – they came to drop their ordinance along the Tyne – and we'd huddle together in the Anderson shelter we had in our backyard, listening to distant booms and the ack-acks clattering in response, watching the burst of the flares. We had to have lessons in how to apply our gas masks and my brothers and I would charge around after each other wearing those frightening, life-saving disguises. I remember the Bevin Boys in our village, men conscripted to help the war effort by toiling in the pit.

My father was in the Home Guard – a role he undertook with gravity, proud of his tin helmet and uniform. He and his colleagues had to prepare for every eventuality, from the prospect of invasion or attack to an enemy plane being shot down. He even had a rifle. He was a skilled first-aider, too, but then it often felt like Dad was superhuman. Aside from his mine work, mending all our shoes, doing the decorating and being a general handyman, he'd also do all our stitching.

My father features prominently in this narrative because he introduced me to football and Newcastle United, but my wonderful mother, Lillian, featured just as prominently in my life. She was a lovely woman, the daughter of a miner, and she spent her entire adult life tending the home and caring for us all. It was thanks to the support, efforts and encouragement of my close-knit family – we didn't have a lot, but what we had, we shared – that I achieved what I did. Not a day goes by when I don't think of my parents and whisper a little word of thanks.

Tynemouth Priory was one of our Sunday destinations. Days at the coast weren't just about gambolling on the beach. We'd go for walks, too, exploring the area. I'm pleased to say that tradition lives on in the Robson family. I'm very proud of my three sons, Paul, Mark and Andrew – the latter has made Tynemouth his home.

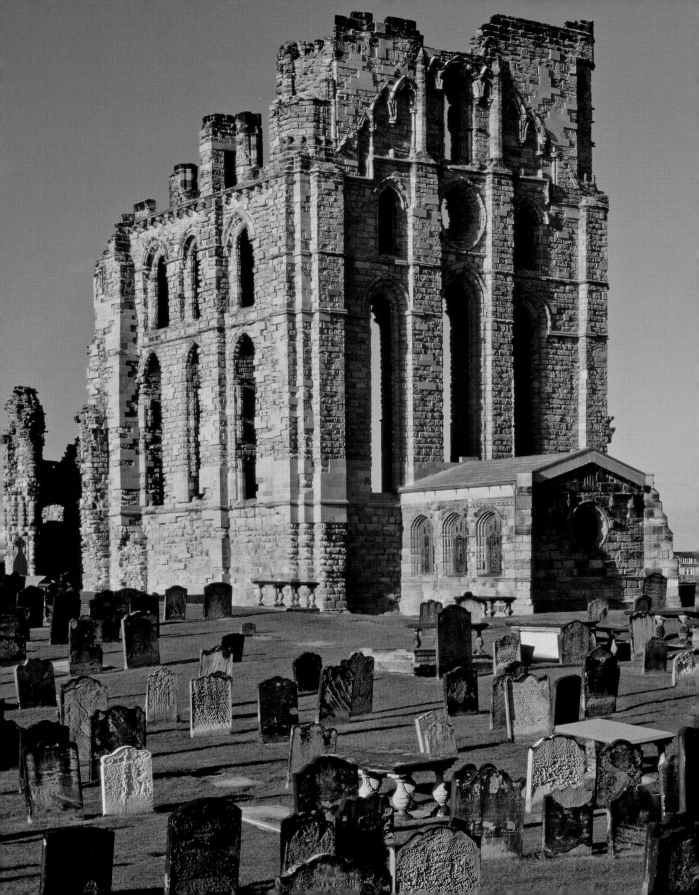

4
THE WORKING WEEK

AN OLD MAN takes his grandson for a walk in their shared place of birth. He points to the shops and offices that have sprung up over the course of his long lifetime, talking about the changes that, for good or bad, have taken place in his town. They stop in front of a supermarket or a multi-storey car park. 'You know, lad,' the elderly gent says, 'I can remember when this was all fields.' Transplant that scene to the North East and, in plenty of places, the conversation would be very different. I could show you green spaces where pit villages once stood, hills instead of slagheaps. I couldn't lead you to many coal mines or shipyards, once the cornerstone of our communities, because the heavy industry that once drove and dominated the region has been decimated. The working landscape and the landscape itself have been transformed beyond recognition since my formative years in Langley Park.

In those days, the phrase people used to describe doing something pointless or superfluous was 'like carrying coals to Newcastle' because the city was built on the dusty diamonds that were hewn from the earth and ferried away. That's a strange, whimsical thought and one tinged with sadness, because the great, harsh era – not that long ago – when coal touched everybody in this part of the world is over. Coal provided for my family and the rest of our village, where most of the men were either miners or reliant on the mine in one way, shape or form. Very few people went away to do other things. The pit was the focal point of our lives. There were colliery bands and outings, we used lumps of coal as makeshift footballs and most of the time we were covered in it, too. We didn't have a bathroom, but every Friday evening Mum would ladle hot water into a tin bath in front of the fire, for my brothers and me. She would wash us and lift us out and my father would dry us. Much of the time we would run around dirty. There was camaraderie beneath the ground and a lot of hardship, too, but that hardship was magnified when the pits were closed down and whole communities evaporated. That life was our heritage.

I'm proud to say that I'm a miner's son, a brother of miners and a miner myself. In fifty-one years in the job, my father, Philip, missed just a single shift at work and that was only because he had a carbuncle on the back of his neck and couldn't twist or turn. Incredible.

Locals may think of the North East as the centre of the universe, but it also a gateway to the world. Newcastle International Airport is a bustling, modern, expanding facility and a major part of our superb transport infrastructure. Working traditions and specialities have evolved since my years down the pit. Here, an air traffic controller keeps a watchful eye on the busy skies.

Steam-powered herring drifters discharge their catch at North Shields fish quay in 1927. It's still a working port and the place to go for the freshest, tastiest fish and fluffy, chunky chips.

LEFT: A miner works the seam in Ashington the year the Second World War erupted. Like this chap, my father was a coal hewer, who fought the Germans with a pick in his hand rather than a rifle. Their work at home was too valuable for them to join the forces. What a hard life that was, down in the dark – probably the hardest of them all. Sometimes my dad would be on his back, hacking away at the coalface, without room to stretch or adjust his position. Your light battery was your lifeline. If it failed, you'd had it. You'd struggle to get back to daylight.

BELOW: Staff and fellow trainees have our picture taken at the Morrison Training Centre, where we were taught the basic skills of the mining industry. Down in that gloomy world, safety was paramount. I learned about travelling to and from the coalface, how important your light and battery were, how to avoid being hit by the coal trucks. A lot of people used to leap on the back of the trucks for a sneaky lift, but that was an invitation to death or serious injury. I'm the smart fellow marked with an x. I've always been a tie man.

ABOVE: Hardship and deprivation have sunk their claws into the North East, where reliance on heavy industry has often brought poverty in its wake. Three years after I was born, two hundred men left Jarrow in order to march to London to protest against unemployment in the shipyards. Here, in October 1936, they stop at a farm near Bedford for corned beef and potatoes.

RIGHT: The Jarrow Crusade passes through Lavendon, then part of Buckinghamshire, on 26 October 1936. The march took place over twenty-two legs and covered some 280 miles. A petition carrying 12,000 names was handed in to the House of Commons by Ellen Wilkinson, the local MP. She described Jarrow at the time as 'utterly stagnant. There was no work.'

LEFT: Stone is tipped away at Horden pit. As much as you tried to leave it beneath the ground, it was impossible not to bring some stone to the surface along with the coal. You'd have to get rid of it somehow. Every mine in every village or town would have a stoneheap or slagheap nearby. Some were like mountains.

ABOVE RIGHT: Coal was not just work, it was life. We used it for the fire, to heat hot water and to cook with – fireplace, boiler, oven. Nobody had gas or electricity in those days. Coal powered everything. Here, men scavenge a slagheap in Newcastle in 1938 for small nuggets of coal amid the stone. In difficult times, those small black slivers could be lifesavers for a poor family. The last pit within the city limits closed in the 1950s. Langley Park was shut down in 1975. The loss of mines was devastating for small communities.

BELOW RIGHT: Steel workers in Jarrow. Mine was more of a coal domain in Langley Park, but when they blew the furnaces at the iron and steel works at Consett – where the steel used for the Blackpool Tower was made – more than nine miles away, the effects would reach our village. My mother would run her finger along our window sills and lift up a thick smudge of red dust. The sky above Consett would glow orange. The works closed in 1980, with the loss of 3,700 jobs.

The Durham Miners' Gala was a real highlight when I was growing up. We never missed it. Each colliery had a banner and a brass band and we'd parade behind them through the centre of Durham as they played their memorable tunes. It was a proud day for all miners. The union and political bigwigs stood on the balcony of the Royal County Hotel, saluting the bands as they passed. Afterwards, we'd congregate on the racecourse for speeches and celebrations. The gala's still going today, although the deep mines are not. The pit was king when I left the North East as a teenager – in 1923, 170,000 miners worked the Durham coalfield. By the time I came back, they were gone.

My dad was very adept at his duties, rising through the ranks to a high position, becoming a deputy, then an overman. My brother Tom was a fitter, but after studying year after year for his diplomas, he got himself qualified and went on to be chief engineer of the National Coal Board in his district. Ron was employed at the Langley Park pit as the coal manager's secretary. I've often remarked that my family bleed black and white and, as well as the obvious footballing connotations, coal must at least be partially responsible for the colour of our blood.

Having left school at fifteen and a half – a conscientious student, but no egghead – I knew it was either football or the pit for me. I couldn't wait until I was seventeen to sign on as a professional sportsman, but I had to be good enough to persuade somebody I was cut out for that life. That thought made me play football with even greater effort. I had a powerful desire to ensure I didn't have to spend the rest of my days underground, but there were no guarantees. Two or three times a week I attended night school to study electrical engineering and technical drawing, but my first job was not running around, hoofing a piece of leather about in the open air, but as an apprentice colliery electrician deep beneath the grass I used to play on. The trappings of my trade were not shorts and boots, but overalls, tin helmet and the alkaline battery I carried on my back. My dad got me the job down the mine and I knew that if I didn't make it on the pitch, then the pitch black would become my second home. To everybody else back then I wasn't Bobby Robson, I was just a kid whose father was one of the deputies of the colliery and quite well known because he'd worked there all his life.

My day would begin at 6.15 a.m. when I was woken by my mum, and thirty minutes later I'd be walking out of the house towards work, ready for a 7 o'clock start, stamping my card to prove what time I'd arrived – not that my parents would have allowed me to be late. I'd get up knowing the commitment and the discipline expected of me. Across the colliery bridge over the railway line I'd tramp, carrying my sandwiches, a bottle of water and my kitbag of tools into the electrical shop. By 7.30 I'd be in the pit-shaft with my marra, my workmate, the qualified electrician, with a bulb fitted on my helmet, because while certain parts of the mine were lit, once you started walking to the coalface, which is where we operated, we were in total darkness. For two or three miles we'd trek along the line, always stooping, in tunnels that were only four or five feet high. The idea was to remove the coal and leave the stone, because the alternative would have cost a fortune, so the roofs were as low as possible.

Beer barrels are washed out at Newcastle brewery. The city is responsible for some notable brews. Referred to as 'Dog' or 'Broon' locally, Newcastle Brown Ale has become one of our most famous exports. Cleaning up afterwards does not look like such a barrel of laughs.

OVERLEAF: Barrel makers at work at 'Arthur's' cooperage on Newcastle's quayside in 1954. The building they're toiling in, one of the oldest in the city, is now the Cooperage pub – where emptying barrels of their contents is more the idea.

Yours truly opening the new bottling plant at Scottish and Newcastle Breweries in 1999.
Nine years later I pressed the plunger on a 250kg cache of explosives to demolish what had
been the home of Newcastle Brown Ale for more than sixty years, creating nearly 10,000
tonnes of rubble in the process. Was it something I said? The site, near St James' Park, has
been sold off to make way for a hotel, student accommodation, offices and apartments,
symbolising the changing face of the city.

Every now and then there would be an opening where you would wait and let the trucks pass, allowing you to sit on your haunches and stretch your back, but comfort was not a regular companion. I've crawled in eighteen inches of cramped space, thousands of feet underground, the length of a football pitch and more, to the coal-cutter at the face, because the machinery had broken down. The coal-cutter did what its name suggests and the men behind shovelled the result on to a conveyor belt that transported it to where the coal could be hefted into tubs and out of the pit. My responsibility was to look after the coal-cutter and fix it when it malfunctioned, to look after the lighting, telephone system, transformers and all the cable work. Like my dad, I'd leave our house white and come back black at about 4.15, for a wash or bath in the family tub and an early supper. My first weekly pay-packet was just over three pounds.

That was my world for a year and a half and I was desperate to get out of it, but those memories and that work ethic stayed with me. Even the thought of our colliery band playing their evocative tunes is enough to make me weep. There was an amazing community spirit down the pit. The comradeship and feeling of honour between the miners, the generosity we displayed to each other and the respect we shared, was intense and real, because down in that murk, trust was the key ingredient. For much of the time, your very existence was in the hands of others. Life or death? For that kind of team, it was a real and daily question. My dad was a Labour man and those principles have stayed with me, because I've seen the value, the absolute necessity, of work, togetherness and unity. For reasons of health, welfare and safety, for the good of our environment, it may not be such a bad thing that the choking dust, those shafts and heaps and mine workings no longer infiltrate our lungs and scar our stunning scenery – the sky above the iron and steel works at Consett used to be clogged with red dust – but I can't help feeling that something important, some unifying force, has been lost in the process. Economically and socially, mine closures took a dreadful toll. I was away during the miners' strike, and when I came back permanently in 1999, the mines had been obliterated. Langley Park was a big colliery, but there's no sign of that now. Even the towering mountain of a coal heap was eventually moved.

The shipyards have gone, too. At the beginning of the twentieth century, more than a quarter of the world's shipping tonnage was built in the North East, where the rivers Tyne, Wear and Tees were at the forefront of the industry, but decline set in, dock closures followed and by the turn of the new millennium, virtually nothing was left.

ABOVE: Before the advent of mobile phones and the internet, trade was much more of a face-to-face operation. Here businessmen find a quiet corner of Newcastle's Commercial Exchange in December 1938 to discuss the volatility of the market. I bet the approach of war and what it would mean for families and livelihoods were uppermost in many minds.

RIGHT: Public wash houses were still quite common in Newcastle in 1955. Everything had to be done by hand in those days. I can picture my mother hurling Dad's filthy pit clothes into a tub of hot water, pounding them with a poss stick, feeding them through a hand mangle and then hanging them on the washing line in our backyard. We'd take our weekly baths in the same tubs.

ABOVE: Marks and Spencer's 'Original Penny Bazaar' in Newcastle's Grainger Market in 1955. Note the sign publicising the sale of 'Athletic Underwear' – perhaps Jackie Milburn was a customer. Open since 1895, the company's oldest branch is still operating to this day and I'm pleased to report that admission is still free.

LEFT: Today, Grainger Market has everything on sale from cards to carpets, meat, fish and vegetables. John Dobson's beautiful building was constructed in 1835 to appease the merchants who had been obliged to move when the centre of the city was redeveloped. It has stood the test of time well.

At Swan Hunter in Wallsend, once one of the most highly regarded ship-building companies, the famous cranes have been sold off and the plant machinery is being dismantled. In sporting terms, there has always been great rivalry between the urban conurbations of Newcastle, Sunderland and Middlesbrough, but they have often been brought together through economic hardship and suffering.

I've had an amazing and privileged career, but just as my roots have always been embedded in the North East, so I've endeavoured to take the region's ethos with me on my travels. My chairman at Ipswich Town, John Cobbold, had a touch of blue blood in his family – his father shot grouse with George VI at Sandringham – and we came from different worlds. One weekend, when we went to play Derby County, I took John and the directors down a mine in Swaddlincote on the morning of the match –

The closure of Swan Hunter, where more than 1,600 ships had been built, and the sale of the cranes that hung over Wallsend, marked the end of another era on Tyneside. When, as a region, we've been so proficient and successful at building ships – and at other heavy construction – and were renowned for it across the world, it's difficult to understand how it can't be viable any longer.

From match of the day to catch of the day – fortunately, the North Sea remains open for business. Here, Amble skipper Stephen Armstrong hands over part of his haul to leading chefs at the second Eat NewcastleGateshead Food Festival in spring 2008. You should have seen the one that got away.

OVERLEAF: With the fading influence of heavy industry, the notion of work has been reinvented. Leisure is now a big employer. Designed by Norman Foster, the Sage Music Centre on the Gateshead side of the river is a magnificent building. I've always admired architects. How on earth do you go about constructing something like this?

early – to give them a glimpse of where I'd come from. They put on overalls, tin hats, knee pads, batteries and lights and descended into the treacherous shade of the shaft. We didn't go right to the coalface, because they wouldn't have managed it, but we took them far enough to hurt. They couldn't believe it. I respected the fact that they went down to see what it was like. All of them said it was the most vivid experience of their lives.

I would have loved to take my Newcastle players down a mine, but I did the next best thing. I took them to Beamish Museum, that marvellous open-air re-creation of north-east life. I made them all go. We used it as an outing and a bonding session, but also to show them what real work was, what industry was like, to demonstrate how fortunate they were. We went everywhere, into the shops, the farm, on the railway and, of course, into the mine. I'm sure some of them wondered how it would make them better players, and one or two may have thought it a waste of time, but others understood and got into the spirit of the exercise. I must say it took me back.

But in spite of all these changes, and the fact that the North East has often been left to fend for itself, this is not a story of unchallenged sorrow. Far from it. What amazes me about Newcastle, the city itself and the area surrounding it, is how the process of reinvention and regeneration has taken place after the loss of the mines, the shipbuilding and so much of what made it a formidable hub of industry. Vibrancy is everywhere.

The business side of things feels very robust – the office, technology and retail sectors have grown enormously, people have jobs and Newcastle itself has become a glamorous leisure destination. Close to the railway station is the Centre for Life, the country's first biotechnology village, and a vital resource for both education and research.

These advances haven't occurred by chance or coincidence. They have taken sweat and time and blood. They have come about through love, effort and respect, through the people of the region. The fact remains that when they closed the pits, demolished the buildings and flattened the stone heaps, when the gates were padlocked and the shafts were sealed, our shared spirit soared too high to be buried in the darkness.

RIGHT: The Newcastle quayside is no longer the sole preserve of warehouses, docks and factories, but the domain of law courts, offices, hotels and fancy bars. Here a group of businessmen enjoy a liquid lunch at the Pitcher and Piano, close to the Millennium Bridge. I've been there.

BELOW: Once it was coals to Newcastle, now its chromosomes. I'm constantly amazed by the extent of our regeneration. New technology and science feature prominently. At the Bioscience Centre, part of the city's Centre for Life, Dr Lyle Armstrong, a member of the Hybrid Embryo Team, goes about his duties.

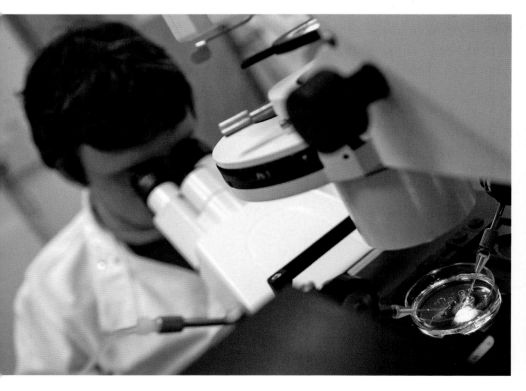

5
LEISURE TIME

To COIN A PHRASE, I've never had much time for free time. Perhaps it's a by-product of my seminal managerial experiences at Ipswich Town, where I ran the club from top to bottom, perhaps it's an ethic that flows through my family line, but I've always thrown myself into my work, usually at the expense of relaxation. Even in my early seventies at Newcastle United, I was first through the gates every morning and the last to leave at night. That isn't a complaint, by the way, just a reflection of character. I adored my job, to the point of obsession. Football wasn't just my profession, it was a vocation, my drug of choice, an addiction that could only be sated by pouring my heart and soul into it. Where do you find those extra percentage points that transform draws into victories? How do you motivate millionaires? Switching off from that was difficult.

During my spell at the club, I was awarded honorary memberships at three local golf clubs. Matfen Hall in Northumberland and two in Co. Durham, Ramside Hall and Brancepeth Castle, were kind enough to grant me that privilege, and although I loved the sport, I seldom played. There was always something that needed attending to, some chore to address, a training-ground routine to think through, or mini-drama to avert. I used to receive eighty letters every day and while Judith, my secretary, could deal with some of them, there were invitations and requests that needed a personal response and I couldn't leave her to do all of it. I tried to answer every one. In my last year at Newcastle, I didn't take a single day off.

Evenings were not my own. Opposing teams would need watching and players scouting, so I'd trek up and down the country to matches. I loved watching the reserves. I've heard stories about Newcastle directors turning up unannounced at second-string fixtures at Kingston Park and failing to spot a single senior member of staff in attendance – which, in my opinion, is nothing short of a disgrace and a gross dereliction of duty. I viewed it as a vital part of my responsibilities. Never missed them. I made my coaches go, too. Tommy Craig was our reserve-team manager and, while I never interfered, I made sure I supported him. On occasion, I would go into the dressing-room at half-time, and would always do so after the game, because it was important for the players to know I was there. Sometimes I'd say a few words.

The Red Arrows decorate the Tyneside skyline during the Great North Run in 2007. What an event this race has become. The most popular and prestigious half-marathon in the world is a genuine showcase for the North East as well as a sporting triumph to rival any other.

Northumberland Plate day at Newcastle Racecourse in Gosforth Park. It always attracts a big crowd of local Thoroughbreds. My family very kindly clubbed together to buy me a horse for my seventy-fifth birthday, but El Bobby is still chasing its maiden victory.

Is it a bird? Is it a plane? Is it the Statue of Liberty? No, it's me, actually, firing the starting pistol for the Great North Run in 2007. That was the second time I'd done it and I've rarely enjoyed a bigger sporting honour. I must have high-fived thousands of runners as they jogged past. I wish they hadn't worn rings – my hand was swollen and black and blue afterwards! I suppose I got to experience a little of the day's pain as well as the pleasure.

ABOVE: I started the New Year's fireworks display in 2003 from the Gateshead Millennium Bridge. A truly wonderful spot, the bridge is a pedestrian link between the two river banks, and a tourist destination in its own right.

OVERLEAF: Out with the old and in with the Newcastle. What an enthralling sight! The North East knows how to party and while we don't need pyrotechnics to sparkle, they certainly help.

The point I'm making is that when Newcastle dispensed with my services, my withdrawal symptoms were deep and severe. I'd been robbed of something that was carved in my soul. At first, acclimatisation was difficult. I have taken on other tasks, including assisting Steve Staunton with the Republic of Ireland for a while and working in the media, while my charitable foundation has snowballed far beyond my original expectations, but in some regards I'm back to where my journey in football began. I'm a fan once more, sitting on the edge of my seat. I can't claim to be first in the queue these days, but my feelings for the game have not wavered, nor those for my club, and my life is still set around the football's contours. I could never stay at home on a Saturday, twiddling my thumbs, if there's a match being played. I was present at St James' Park on that heady evening when Kevin Keegan returned for the third time, and I felt the excitement spread through the stadium. The chap in front of me spent the entire evening with his back to the FA Cup replay against Stoke City that was taking place – he was too busy gawping at Kevin! He was absolutely ecstatic. It was as if he was watching an astronaut return from the moon. After a lifetime in the game, football has become my pastime. In some ways, I acknowledge that it always was.

Family has consistently been my release, tugging me down to earth after a pleasing win or building me up when troubles were pressing in on me. My time in their company remains precious. My other interests have been crammed in around them, but some are dear to me and sometimes the two combine. In the spring of 2008, I was waiting for the results of a medical scan. I'm in the process of fighting cancer for the fifth time and I was due to hear what developments there had been. I was a bit worried, to be honest, and I didn't know what kind of news I'd be getting. As it transpired, it was as good as I could have hoped for. There had been no further growth. As she always has been, Elsie was by my side.

ABOVE: Bobby Thompson was a great northern comedian and one of my father's favourites. 'The Little Waster', rarely without his trademark fag, flat cap and stripy jumper, famously incurred the wrath of the taxman. He never watered down his accent for the sake of his act, quite the opposite. It was integral to it. 'There was a knock at the door last Wednesday mornin'. She says, "This is Anne from Littlewoods." I says, "God bless ya. I've won the treble chance?" She says, "No, your wife's up for shoplifting." '

RIGHT: As Newcastle United manager, I presided over plenty of it, but St James' Park has rich competition when it comes to providing quality drama. The Tyne Theatre and Opera House on Westgate Street is another of the city's stunning venues, over 140 years old, a Grade I listed building and a treasure of the music-hall era. Described as the world's oldest working Victorian theatre, its long-term future has been safeguarded now that it has been bought by Newcastle City Council.

Grant, Fred Astaire and Ginger Rogers, Joseph Cotten and James Stewart, and have an ice cream at the interval. *An American in Paris* starring Gene Kelly was a big favourite. Elsie and I adopted 'Our Love is Here to Stay' as our song.

It was just as well. I met Elsie when I was eighteen and married her at twenty-two, but for most of the intervening time we were courting from a distance. She was training to be a nurse at Sunderland infirmary and I was at Fulham. We wrote to each other religiously and saw each other in the summer – when I'd play cricket for the village – and winter holidays. We'd sit in the living room, listening to music, or go for walks together. By then, her brother owned a little Ford car, which he let us borrow once or twice, so outings were a possibility. In between times, I'd collect sixpences, walk to the telephone kiosk next to Craven Cottage and ring her at the hospital, either when her shift had just finished or when it was about to start. Eventually, after we were engaged, Elsie's parents allowed her to visit me at my digs in London. We stayed in separate rooms, of course, because there was no tomfoolery in those days. And, in any case, I had a proper look-out landlady.

In those lonely months of solo living, I'd search out company on the bookshelf. I've always wished for more time to spend reading. I just think it's a fantastic pastime. I've enjoyed the novels of Wilbur Smith, the historical fiction of Leon Uris and James Michener. I dip into the military histories of John Keegan, which fascinate me, and as you might expect, my study is groaning with biographies and autobiographies of famous sportsmen and women, many of them friends. I'm still dying to read Kitty Kelley's biography of Sinatra.

I loved seeing the big shows in London, a fondness that doubtless grew from the annual family tradition of going to the pantomime at Newcastle's Theatre Royal. My parents were humble people with five children to support, but they certainly did their best for us. I was usually the most vociferous of the brothers, booing and hissing at Cinderella's Ugly Sisters. Like most of the surrounding area, Newcastle's Theatre Royal is a stunning building and the ritzy interior made a deep impression on young eyes. I've been there since my return to the city.

The theatre has hosted the Royal Shakespeare Company on its tours for more than thirty years and those people who, without thinking, paint the North East as culturally lacking are speaking from ignorance. In response, I suggest a stroll around the Baltic Centre for Contemporary Art, which is housed in a renovated flour mill and has a fine restaurant on the top floor.

Michael Owen demonstrates a different type of ball skill at the Seve Trophy Pro-Am at Wynyard Golf Club. Many footballers love to ease the pressures of performing in the Premier League with a round of golf and the North East has some of the most beautiful courses in the country.

Two Geordie heroes, Alan Shearer and Steve Harmison, the Durham and England pace bowler, enjoy a round together. Steve – the 'Ashington Express' – is passionate about Newcastle United. Jackie Milburn and the Charlton brothers are other famous natives of his town, which has a proud mining history.

Miles Tunnicliff tees off at the Great North Open at De Vere Slaley Hall in 2002. This demanding championship course has a luscious setting. From mature woodland to links courses,`the North East has got them all.

With the Laing Art Gallery, the Sage, the delicious eateries and the cinemas all close by, if you live in or around Newcastle, finding something to engage the mind or tax the body is never a problem.

Football will always be the mainstay of our sporting calendar, but since my retirement I've whiled away many an enjoyable day at Durham County Cricket Club, where I'm an honorary member. I go when I can. I saw the one-day international there between England and New Zealand in the summer of 2008 and enjoyed a nice chat on the chairman's balcony with Jacob Oram, who is a mad-keen Arsenal fan. I love swapping anecdotes and experiences with people from different disciplines. I'm predominantly a football and cricket lover, but I've been to watch the Newcastle Falcons rugby union team. While I was United manager, I gladly gave permission for Jonny Wilkinson and Co. to use our covered training facilities when the north-east weather was at its harshest. Basketball, ice hockey and athletics also compete for attention in our sports-mad area.

For my seventy-fifth birthday, my sons and friends clubbed together to buy me a horse. They chose a very clever name for it, El Bobby, with the El representing Elsie and also tipping its hat to my stint at Barcelona. I go to Newcastle races every now and again and the racecourse tie is on regular rotation in my wardrobe.

Unfortunately, I'm physically unable to play golf any more, which is a big disappointment, because I was beginning to love the game. Straightening my hook and slice was something I was very much looking forward to. Like gardening, it's an activity that clears the mind of clutter. You forget about everything else and concentrate on hitting that little ball, playing the course and playing your opponent. I never had lessons. I only ever had time to play, not practise, but there are some beautiful courses spread right across the North East, from links courses set in dunes, to green gems hidden away in the countryside. It's one of the advantages of the area.

I've twice been the starter for the Great North Run and what a thrill, what a sight, that was. Around 50,000 athletes congregate in Newcastle every year for the world's most popular half-marathon, which has become a wonderful regional showpiece and a significant fundraiser for grateful charities. When I fired the starting pistol in 2007, I began slapping hands with the runners as they bounded past. It took me three days to recover, but I wouldn't have missed it for the world.

Jonny Wilkinson in action for the Newcastle Falcons. We should be very proud to have had two England Number 10s from different sporting disciplines in our midst. Like Michael Owen, Jonny is a good boy and a solid character, with a reputation for perfectionism.

6
HEART OF THE CITY

ABOVE THE BANKS of the curving river, architectural jewels jockey for attention. Steep boulevards stretch down to the pulsing water, straddled by bridges of differing design and dimensions. St James' Park, a constant reminder of football's daily presence, looms above Georgian masterpieces, chipped out of golden stone. As far as dramatic vistas are concerned, Newcastle upon Tyne compares with the best of them, but this is not a dry and dusty city. Graceful buildings house cafés, bars and restaurants. Statues look down on busy shoppers. History surrounds us and the old traditions of heavy industry inspire us, but the modern has been embraced with equal vigour. This place is alive.

I've lived in capital cities, from London to Lisbon, and I've travelled the world extensively, my days with club and country leading me to Asia, the Americas and Africa, but Newcastle stands up to all comparisons. 'It's grim up north,' used to be the saying, but seldom from the mouths of those who take the trouble to visit us. It's true that the region was once the engine of the world, digging and dispatching coal, forging iron and steel, sending ships to distant shores, but those smokestacks and slagheaps always co-existed with splendour. We are touched by natural beauty in the shape of our empty coastline, green countryside and blissful dales, but in our midst are a bevy of man-made wonders.

Anybody who has stood in the shadow of Grey's Monument and gazed southwards will know what I'm talking about. It's not a view you would associate with belching chimneys or factory floors. Sir John Betjeman, the former poet laureate, summed it up rather nicely: 'As for the curve of Grey Street, I shall never forget seeing it to perfection, traffic-less on a misty Sunday morning. Not even Regent Street, even old Regent Street, London, can compare with that descending subtle curve.' In 2002, Grey Street was voted the best in the UK by BBC Radio 4 listeners. I can't fault their judgement, except to ask what took them so long.

Every town and city has its own character, but it is the combination of qualities that makes Newcastle so compelling – a giant of a football club in its central setting, the working heritage, the snaking river and some of the finest architecture you could ever hope to see. The aspect I particularly love is the dynamic relationship between the old and the new. On the Gateshead

The River God Tyne. Attached to the exterior of the Civic Centre, David Wynne's 1968 sculpture, cast in bronze, is based on representations of England's main rivers exhibited at Somerset House in London. The original mask had blazing coal, a pick and shovel and nets carved on its head to symbolise Tyneside's early industries. There couldn't have been enough space for a football!

side of the river, the Baltic Flour Mill is now a modern art gallery; on the Newcastle side, law-courts, hotels and offices adorn a quayside where warehouses once thrived. Two-hundred-year-old edifices house Indian restaurants and fashionable boutiques. The structures are grand, but there is no sense of self-importance. It's something that other places simply don't have. To people bustling into Eldon Square or racing to work, I'd offer a humble recommendation – glance upwards. You're surrounded by palaces. As a youngster, dashing from the bus to Fenwick's for a ham roll and a cuppa and blinded by football, I was barely aware of what I was passing, other than that the scale and the grandeur were of a different dimension from anything in my village, but I've got to know more about it in recent years. You can just stand in the city centre, look around you and marvel.

For those splendid visions, we have some visionaries to be grateful to. In the 1820s, '30s and '40s, John Dobson, the architect, and Richard Grainger, the builder – with notable contributions from others – reshaped much of Newcastle's city centre. Between them, either individually or in partnership, they planned and constructed Grey Street – named after Earl Grey, the nineteenth-century prime minister – old Eldon Square, the Grainger Market, the Central Arcade, the Theatre Royal, Central Station and far too many others to mention. Newcastle must have been choking in dust during those decades of building work, but the effort was worthwhile, because the legacy Dobson and Grainger left for us is still being appreciated and enjoyed. I can think of other cities that have pulsating pockets of activity or beautiful architecture, but very few with the mix that Newcastle can offer.

The Central Station, with the lazy curl of the track and high ceilings, is a particular favourite of mine. Dobson had plans for an intricate exterior, which was never built, but the outside still looks like the entrance to a stately home or museum. Inside, the iron roofing gives the impression of movement and it was an incredible sight to see thick plumes of steam rising from the engines. I think my fondness for the station may be because it reminds me of all the travelling I've done since I first stepped on to the rattler to Whitley Bay and Tynemouth. And also because it makes me think about coming back.

For similar reasons, the Tyne Bridge holds a special place in the hearts of most Geordies. Once that famous green steel arch comes into view, belonging to Newcastle as recognisably as Brown Ale and black-and-white stripes, they can relax. They're home. Given the importance of the river in our history, the vital role it played in the movement of goods and people, it is only right that people have such an emotional attachment to the Tyne Bridge.

This is the castle that was once new. If United's defence was this stout, they would never concede another goal. The Castle Keep was erected by Henry II between 1168 and 1178 and is now open to the public.

Built in 1247 by Henry III, the Black Gate was the final part of the city's castle defences to be constructed, forming an additional protective barbican to the north gate. In later years, a public house was opened there, while by the early nineteenth century, the Black Gate had become a slum tenement housing sixty people. It is now the home of the country's oldest provincial antiquarian society.

People know about Durham, York and Edinburgh, but when they consider Newcastle, perhaps they don't automatically think of the majesty on display here, but majesty is the right word. I just think this vista is stunning, eye-catching and attractive – rare, too. You don't find its equivalent in many cities. From Grey's Monument, Grey Street curls away to the left and Grainger Street strikes off to the right.

(Inset) Earl Grey was an interesting chap and enlightened for his time. Born in Northumberland, his family's ancestral seat was at Howick Hall. He entered parliament at the age of twenty-two. As Whig Prime Minister, he famously oversaw the passage of the 1832 Reform Act and secured the abolition of slavery throughout the British Empire. Earl Grey tea was named after him, too.

RIGHT: Grey Street is my favourite Newcastle thoroughfare, with its exquisite bend towards the river, the imposing buildings and pavements made of Portland stone. William Gladstone, no less, termed it England's finest street, and who am I to disagree?

LEFT: Another of John Dobson and Richard Grainger's masterpieces, old Eldon Square was affected when the modern shopping centre, which bears the same name, was built. Two sides of the square were destroyed but what remains is still notable, with its war memorial depicting St George and the Dragon. It's a place in which to congregate and reflect.

OVERLEAF: Quite why anybody would wish to leave Newcastle is beyond me, but for those who do, this city of bridges offers a wide choice of crossings to the south. You can see three of them here. The Tyne Bridge is an emblem of the city, but everybody has their own favourite. It's always a treat to see the Swing Bridge swivel, while the blinking eye of the Millennium Bridge in the distance is reserved for pedestrians and cyclists.

ABOVE: Each era hails its own progress and leaves it own legacy. When the Central Station was built in the 1840s, it took the place of a large section of Newcastle's ancient city walls. While that would be regarded as sacrilege now, John Dobson's magnificent structure has come to be recognised as an historical landmark in its own right. I hope future generations will feel the same way. I've always loved it.

ABOVE RIGHT: The interior of Central Station is definitely equal to the first impressions gained outside. The curve of the trains as they sweep down the platforms is amazing. Given that the birth of the public railway took place in the North East, it's only proper that we should have a regal station – Queen Victoria and Prince Albert presided over its official opening on 29 August 1850.

RIGHT: Clean, efficient and reliable, the Tyne and Wear Metro system connects Newcastle with the coast, to the expanding international airport and to Sunderland. Forty million journeys are taken on it each year, so the Metro has been a real boon for the region, and it's appreciated by footsore supporters of both local football clubs.

The Central Arcade, with its glass roof, gleaming tiles and hanging baskets, presents a unique visual experience. J.G. Windows, the music shop, has been purveying its tuneful wares in this Richard Grainger-built edifice since 1908, while the Tourist Information Centre is a more recent tenant.

LEFT: A taste of the Orient can be found on our doorstep. Newcastle's Chinatown runs the length of Stowell Street and is crammed with restaurants and shops, complete with gleaming sights and mouth-watering aromas of the Far East. Even the telephone boxes have pagoda roofs. Newcastle's first Chinese restaurant opened in Scotswood in 1949.

RIGHT: In Eldon Square and Northumberland Street – and with the Metro Centre in close proximity – those in need of retail therapy can fill their boots while emptying their purses with abandon. Eldon Square was opened in 1976. This is a picture of the Mirror Gallery in the exclusive Eldon Garden.

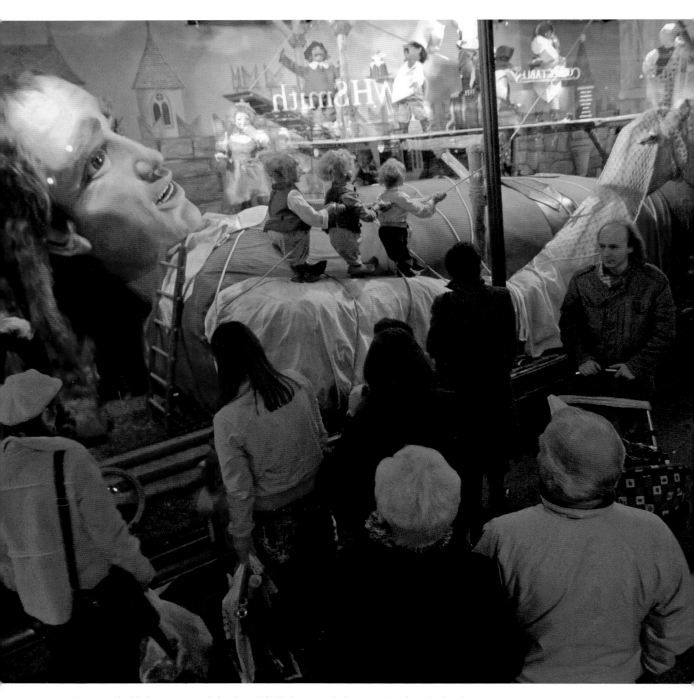

Young and old cluster around the Fenwick Christmas windows on Northumberland Street. With a nod to children's favourites – 2006 featured scenes from *Gulliver's Travels* – the windows have become an annual Newcastle tradition during the winter holidays.

Northumberland Street is bordered by inviting shops, banks and cafés. Fenwick's, opened in 1882, is still going strong and draws huge crowds every Christmas, when its windows are decorated with festive themes. Bainbridge and Binns were the other big department stores I remember from my youth. Eldon Square offers retail therapy in the guise of more than 150 outlets.

I never had to sell Newcastle as a place to any player I wanted to sign when I was United manager. Not a single time. Many of the new stadiums that have been opened in the last ten years or so have been good for football, offering a safer and more conducive environment for families and children, and sometimes clubs need to break from the past, but the danger is that they lose an element of their soul. For that reason, among others, I'm delighted St James' Park remains intact. You can feel the lifeblood swirling around it and I'm sure the players can, too. Within moments, you're in the heart of the city, where you can find anything you could wish for – architecture, cinemas, nightlife, theatres, music, restaurants and shops. It's not clogged up with traffic, yet the A1 is close by, there's a mainline station and an international airport within easy distance. The coast and countryside beckon.

Districts outside the centre have their own identities and qualities. The Ralph Erskine-designed Byker Wall, home to 9,500 people, has been placed on UNESCO's list of outstanding twentieth-century buildings and in 2007 was given a Grade II listing. Wallsend has a proud shipbuilding heritage but, as its name suggests, was also the eastern end of Hadrian's Wall. Jesmond is a buzzing suburb, favoured by students and professionals, Gosforth has desirable homes and a busy high street. There are parks and denes – the rugged oasis of the Town Moor is within comfortable walking distance – housing estates and tower blocks, terraces and maisonettes, highways and avenues. Amid all the beauty of water, steel, concrete and turf you can feel the drumming beat of a place locked in the fascinating cycle of work and play.

OVERLEAF: Northumberland Street was a busy road when, as a boy, I made my fortnightly visits to St James' Park via Fenwick's restaurant. Now it's clogged with human traffic only. The pedestrianisation of Newcastle's signature shopping boulevard has made that activity far more of a treat – or so Elsie tells me.

7
HEARTBEAT OF THE CITY

COAL MAY BE OBSOLETE, but Newcastle and its hinterland has always embraced an alternative source of energy, for this is a place fuelled by football. Just as the pit was once the hub of life for much of the North East, so St James' Park perches like a colossus in the centre of the city, where it occupies and entrances its citizens. The influence of the club, its history and its present, pervades everything, sometimes in a highly visible way. The restaurants, bars, shops and conference facilities contained within the imposing stadium confirm it as a notable employer, for instance, but there are less mundane, less tangible aspects to it. The ghosts of heroes surround you, the spectre of daring deeds hangs in the air. When the team is faring well or badly, the atmosphere of the place lifts or sours accordingly, and whether you talk to taxi drivers, waiters or shop staff, everybody has a tale to tell. It can be suffocating or it can be liberating. Sometimes you can never quite be sure. I love it.

Newcastle is a football city and a city of footballers. Some of the finest players this country has produced either grew up in Newcastle's shadow or followed the team. From the club's two most potent post-war goalscorers, Jackie Milburn and Alan Shearer, to Paul Gascoigne, Chris Waddle and Peter Beardsley, to the Charlton brothers and Bryan Robson, the breadth of the talent to have originated in the region over the decades is staggering. You may have noticed a theme in the list I've mentioned. The Charltons never played for Newcastle – although Jack later managed them – and nor did Bryan, while Alan signed for the club when he was almost twenty-six and had already established himself as an England international. How did he get to Southampton? How did that happen? Even Peter was released by the club as a teenager, while Steve Bruce and Michael Carrick were ignored. Look at those players – big, big players – who were allowed to leave the North East. It should never have happened and the trend must be stopped, but Newcastle have not always been assiduous in the way they nurture the talent on their doorstep.

There are personal reasons for my passion, because I was also one of those émigrés. As a kid, I had the chance to join Newcastle United but I turned them down. Even now, I can scarcely believe it. I was mad about the club, as was my dad, and watched my idols play there every other week.

Saluting the Toon Army's foot-soldiers after a match at St James' Park – I look happy, so we must have won. I'd enjoy reading the newspapers when that was the case, but satisfaction would linger only until Monday morning. Then it was gone and you were back to work. Win or lose, you had to put it to one side and prepare your team for the next challenge.

ABOVE: This is the stadium as I first encountered it. The match against Huddersfield Town in 1954 comes from a period when Newcastle had a swashbuckling side of FA Cup kings. The crowd and the ground look very different now, but the words to the 'Blaydon Races' haven't changed and the passion remains the same.

LEFT: Spectators at St James' in 1938 – no replica shirts on display, but hats on every head. Football continued when war broke out the following year, but in a much-reduced format, with local leagues and guest players. Jackie Milburn even appeared in the red-and-white stripes of Sunderland during the conflict. I saw my first game at that time, beginning a love affair that would never die.

RIGHT: Alec Mutch, pictured here, was Newcastle's assistant trainer when they tried to sign me. I was fifteen and a bit of a prodigy in my village. They couldn't get my signature until I was seventeen, but they were aware of me. Unfortunately, their courtship wasn't as avid as Fulham's, whose manager travelled all the way to Langley Park to meet my parents, and the chance to play for my boyhood idols disappeared. Look at the boots Alec is laying out on the pitch. They had big solid leather toecaps for protection – if you were kicked with one of them, it could break your leg. By comparison, boots are more like slippers today.

BELOW: Although I was born the following year, the 1932 FA Cup final was my introduction to Newcastle United. My father would regale the family with stories of his marathon journey to support the team. Newcastle beat Arsenal courtesy of a disputed Jack Allen goal, when Jimmy Richardson's cross was judged to have stayed in play. My dad, all 5ft 8in. of him, was standing right at the other end of Wembley Stadium, but he was adamant that the goal was legitimate! He had won a competition in the *Evening Chronicle* for a ticket, travelled to London by train on Friday evening, enjoyed a tour of London on an open-topped charabanc the following morning and ate lunch at a Lyons Corner House. He returned to Langley Park, exhausted but elated, on the Sunday.

LEFT: What a fantastic photograph! Joe Harvey, the captain, introduces members of the Newcastle team to George VI before the 1951 Cup final. Those are the players I remember most vividly. Wor Jackie is shaking the King's hand. Jack Fairbrother, the goalkeeper, is half-hidden, with Bobby Cowell, Bob Corbett and Bobby Mitchell also on view. I went to all three triumphant Wembley finals in the 1950s. The stadium felt like a second home to Novocastrians.

BELOW: Preparing to hail the conquering heroes at Central Station in 1951. 'Welcome Hyem Canny Lads' the sign reads. That was exactly how Gazza used to speak: 'Ahm gannin' hyem.' Don Howe, my coach with England, used to ask me: 'What did he just say?' Bryan Robson, Chris Waddle, Peter Beardsley and I were often the only people who could understand Paul. The rest of the squad were just baffled.

ABOVE: George Robledo, the Chilean inside forward, heads the winning goal past the Arsenal goalkeeper, George Swindon, in the 1952 FA Cup final. George and his brother Ted both appeared for United that day, the first time more than one foreign player had appeared in a Cup final XI. After his retirement, Ted went to work on an oil tanker, but the end of his life remains shrouded in mystery. It was said that he was thrown overboard and drowned, but his body was never discovered.

LEFT: The 1950s were the champagne decade for Newcastle, although the beverage of choice looks more like beer. Victorious at Wembley for the second year running, Newcastle players and staff celebrate in the dressing-room after beating Arsenal 1–0. The old stadium has not been such a happy place for the club in recent times.

RIGHT: Jackie Milburn leaps to head the opening goal in the 1955 FA Cup final. Barely forty-five seconds had elapsed, making it the quickest Cup final goal on record until Chelsea's Roberto di Matteo eclipsed it in 1997. Jackie wasn't particularly renowned for his aerial ability, but he had all the time in the world to pick his spot here. Just look at Manchester City's marking, or rather the lack of it! Dear me, if that happened in today's game, the centre half would be left to rot in the reserves for a season.

BELOW: I got married in 1955 and Elsie accompanied me to watch Newcastle's third final in five years. I bought a pair of tickets for three shillings and sixpence each – not that Elsie, bless her, saw much of the match. She is so tiny that the only time she glimpsed the ball was when it was hoofed into the air. The celebrations were memorable, however – when Jimmy Scoular received the Cup from the Queen, nobody would have dreamt that Newcastle would fail to win another domestic honour that century. In 2008, it was me doing the honours, handing over that beautiful old pot to Harry Redknapp's Portsmouth. As a manager, I won the FA Cup with Ipswich.

ABOVE: Terry Hibbert runs with the ball during the
1974 FA Cup final in a short-lived moment of
Newcastle superiority. A Liverpool side featuring
Kevin Keegan, who scored twice, won comfortably.
Wembley no longer felt like a family friend. United
would lose there to Manchester City in their only
appearance at a League Cup final and then to
Arsenal and Manchester United in the FA Cup finals
of 1998 and 1999. Sir Alex Ferguson's team would
also thrash them 4–0 in the 1996 Community
Shield. Geordies have always had deep feelings for
the FA Cup, but many must have been secretly
pleased when the old Wembley was torn down.

RIGHT: Even in disappointment – and there has been
too much of that – United fans will support their
team, and in 1974 they showed their solidarity with
their defeated heroes. Through thin and thinner,
they show admirable loyalty. Imagine how many
would pile on to the streets if there was a trophy
to celebrate. The revelry would last for weeks.

I used to loiter at St James' Park after matches to collect autographs, but instead of doing the obvious thing and grabbing the opportunity to join Newcastle, I agreed to go to Fulham in distant London. Can I explain this aberration? Well, yes I can. Whereas Newcastle sent their scout to Langley Park to ask if I would sign forms with them, Fulham's manager, Bill Dodgin Snr, made the long trek to our house to sit in my mother's living room and wouldn't leave until he'd secured my signature. That commitment made a deep impression. He persuaded my mum and dad, and me, that Fulham was the perfect club for my development – not as big as Arsenal, maybe, but their youth policy was bright and inventive – and that as long as I was prepared to knuckle down, I would get in the team. He convinced me that Fulham was a better deal for me than staying with big-spending Newcastle, where young, local players were either ignored or struggled to make the grade.

So I signed for Fulham, all because the manager was prepared to sit in my mother's living room. Bill's influence stayed with me when I embarked on my managerial career. You had to go after the players you wanted, to show them and their families that you cared about them and had their best interests at heart. Players will often sign for specific managers and if you're a big manager at a big club, you won't fail too many times, but you can't build a house, whether grand or humble, without solid foundations. I did play at my favourite stadium, but only in opposition colours. They were still important occasions for me and I'd be scrounging tickets for weeks beforehand in order to satisfy the demand from family and friends.

Too many youngsters are permitted to slip through the net – the state of the youth system was a genuine concern when I returned to manage Newcastle – and the list of those who have blossomed elsewhere is almost criminal. Bobby and Jack Charlton were from mining stock, from the pit town of Ashington, and Jackie Milburn was their mother's cousin – World Cup winners, the pair of them, but not in the stripes of Newcastle. I represented my country alongside Bobby and both of us played on that famous day at Wembley in 1961 when we beat Scotland 9–3. He was playing outside left, but he was equally adept with either foot – I never knew whether he was better with his left or right. He had a wonderful feint, was good in the air, had the ability to beat people, was a great long passer but could play it short, and he could cross the ball, come inside or go outside. It was a formidable package.

Bobby went on to become a legendary figure at Manchester United and so did another guy, a Co. Durham boy like me, who grew up supporting the black and whites. Bryan Robson's early hero was Wyn Davies, that towering Gallowgate target-man, but after trials at Newcastle, among other clubs, he left for West Bromwich Albion. Crazy!

Bryan had everything. He is one of the top people I ever encountered in terms of attitude, toughness, desire, enthusiasm and commitment. What a bloody warrior, what a captain – the best I had as England manager, without a doubt. What about this for a list of qualities – bravery in the tackle, adept at repossessing the ball and getting forward, aerial courage, scoring goals, creating them and preventing them.

He was inspirational, as tough as teak, and I never saw him flinch from a challenge, so much so that he would bring agony on himself. Malcolm Allison once said that Bryan had to be less kamikaze in what he did otherwise his career would be truncated through injury, but if he hadn't embraced that kind of hazard with his eyes open, he wouldn't have been our Bryan Robson; he would have been ordinary. He wasn't stupid, but nor was he afraid of anything, and that put him on a higher plane than everyone else. Call it a winner's mentality, but he had it in spades.

PREVIOUS SPREAD: Kevin Keegan says his farewells to the Toon Army after his last match as a player in May 1984. We fell out when I was England manager, but I'm pleased to say that we've long since patched up our differences. Kevin has become a real Pied Piper to the club's supporters. As a player, he was terrific, a bundle of energy who maximised every ounce of his talent.

Kevin with his trusty lieutenant and Newcastle's great survivor, Terry McDermott. This photograph was taken in their early days on the coaching scene – both are now fully paid-up members of management's grey-hair club. At the beginning of 2008, their partnership was re-established. If they replicate a fraction of their previous achievements, they will have done better than most.

Lift-off on Gallowgate. Having stabilised the club, Kevin steered Newcastle to a stunning promotion at the conclusion of his first full season in management. Playing stylish, attacking football, the team returned to the big time where, notwithstanding the odd scare, they've remained ever since. The ground would soon be refurbished, and a season-ticket sell-out, as Kevin persuaded his board to back him heavily in the transfer market. After years in the wilderness, supporters could dream again.

LEFT: One of the most dashing members of Kevin's team of 'Entertainers', David Ginola was a lovely player, with real star quality. Right-footed, but adept on the left, the Frenchman offered great control, a clever wriggle and Gallic flair. He could dart inside, cross the ball and hit venomous shots. I thought seriously about bidding for David when I was manager at Barcelona, before moving on to alternative targets. He loved the big stage. You can't change history, but I've often wondered how he would have fared under me at the Nou Camp.

RIGHT: Darren Peacock, the pony-tailed centre half, towered above Manchester United's Eric Cantona in October 1996. Earlier that year, Newcastle had lost out in an epic duel for the title, but a measure of revenge was gained in a spectacularly lopsided victory at St James' Park. The club released a video to commemorate the famous scoreline, calling it 'Howay 5–Oh'.

One of the best nights in Newcastle's recent history was also one of my greatest disappointments, because I wasn't there, having moved upstairs to become Barcelona's director of signings. Louis van Gaal was in charge when the Catalan club were drawn against Newcastle in the Champions League in 1997. I would have loved to have been there, but Louis didn't invite me and I didn't think it was right to invite myself, so I stayed away. Consolation came in travelling the world for a year on a princely salary, scouting for players. Newcastle won 3–2, with Faustino Asprilla scoring a memorable hat-trick.

In the dressing-room before a match, once I'd delivered my team-talk, Bryan would pick up the ball and say, 'Right, are we ready lads? Let's welly this lot.' He was magnificent. When he was in the team, I always felt we had a chance of winning, and when he wasn't there, there'd be a weakness, something lacking. He played ninety times for England, but must have missed another thirty games through injury. We had to send him home twice from World Cup finals. You wonder what might have been.

Bryan was never able to pull on the shirt he grew up idolising, but, like Alan Shearer before me, I was to get another chance with my home-town club. After spells abroad with PSV Eindhoven, Sporting Lisbon, FC Porto and Barcelona, I'd come back to England to enjoy my retirement, but when the 1999–2000 season started and I wasn't gainfully employed for the first time in decades, I hated my fidgety freedom. Once before, when I'd been in Spain, I'd had to reject Newcastle's advances, although my options at the time were limited. What a lot of people don't know is that there was a punitive clause in my contract stating that if I walked out on Barcelona, the money they'd paid me would have to be reimbursed. Apparently, Barcelona sack you, but you don't sack Barcelona! In any case, I hadn't joined such a mammoth club in order to leave. I had joined them to have a right good go.

I never thought the opportunity would arise again, but when Ruud Gullit submitted his resignation, I looked around at my competitors and while I was worried that my age might count against me, I thought I had a sniff. Coming home was a dream. I wish my father had been alive to see it, because he would have been mesmerised. My family, my children were so excited, because it was our club, a big club, and the club I'd always loved. Despite that heritage, it was never easy, always challenging. It was an enormous job. The club had no academy – they hadn't taken up the licence – and the training facilities were absolutely dreadful. In fact, disgraceful would be a more apt description. Most other clubs had moved in the right direction, but Newcastle had done nothing – the manager didn't even have his own office and there was no chief scout. We'd been left behind, so I had to fight to get improvements and fight I did. I shudder to think about how much young talent slithered through the fingers of a club with grandiose ambitions, enormous support and those quicksand foundations.

I knew about the size of the club and the fervour of its support. I knew it was a hotbed, that the fans were vociferous, with great enthusiasm and greater expectations, and with a fabulous tribal loyalty that guaranteed passion through thick and thin. But Newcastle were a long way from being in the top six.

ABOVE: Day one in the Newcastle dug-out involved an away trip to Chelsea. I'm bellowing out orders and look my usual animated self, which is more than I can say for the bench behind me – they're half asleep! On my first appearance as an English club manager since 1982, I was afforded a warm, spine-tingling reception by both sets of fans. Graham Poll, the referee, was less accommodating. We were denied a clear penalty and lost 1–0.

LEFT: At my unveiling as Newcastle manager in 1999, I was concerned that people would focus on my date of birth rather than my pedigree, but I was fit, healthy and ready for a challenge. How I wish my dad had been alive to see me take control of the team we both followed so avidly. I didn't quite get the crowd that Alan Shearer or Michael Owen attracted, but I've had few prouder moments – when I looked into those faces, it was my father I saw. It's difficult to explain the sheer thrill of leading your boyhood club.

LEFT: Alan Shearer and I share the limelight, and a laugh, at a pre-match press conference in Chester-le-Street. The club didn't have its own training facilities when I arrived. That was something I was eager to rectify. I quite enjoyed my tussles with the media. I didn't seek publicity, but I recognised that good communication with fans went a long way towards being successful.

ABOVE: Out on the training pitch in my club tracksuit, I could do what I loved most. I was bloody good at it, too. Here I am sharing the daily ritual of banter alongside Kieron Dyer, Steve Harper and Robert Lee. I never understood how Ruud Gullit could have omitted Rob from his squad, although I guessed it was a political decision relating to his close friendship with Alan. I just saw him towards the end of his career, but Rob was a great player.

OVERLEAF: The game you dared not lose was the one against Sunderland. Here their supporters enjoy the sublime view at St James' Park. Not all Newcastle managers have appreciated the significance of games against our nearest rivals, but as a local lad I understood what it meant to the people. My record was decent, too.

The cathedral choir in song. St James' in full voice and at full capacity is a daunting sound and inspirational sight and should be a significant advantage to Newcastle players. Those wonderful fans have to be given something to cheer about, however. He will live or die by results, but that's where a manager comes in. To play the right type of football, he has to find the right type of players.

For my seventieth birthday, my office at Newcastle was festooned with cards, which were kindly put on display by Judith, my secretary. I had hundreds of them. I've always believed that age is just a number. I felt young and fit, like I could go on forever. I thought of myself as Tarzan. The club's directors had other ideas for me. So, it transpired, did cancer.

At times Duncan and Alan were unplayable, the perfect combination, holding up the ball, heading it, and allowing Gary Speed to burst through the middle. Phew!

Pace was something I loved in my team and with Craig Bellamy and Kieron Dyer in harness, we were assured of it. Another favourite match was when we beat Feyenoord 3–2 to qualify for the second phase of the Champions League. We had led 2–0, the Dutch club had clawed their way back to 2–2 and suddenly the game was on a knife-edge; whichever team won was through. Bellamy's ninetieth-minute goal got us there. The club's moneymen were happy to stump up for a drink for the players that night, which wasn't always the case. I remember some great games against Leeds United, when Leeds were Leeds, and I recall beating Arsenal 3–1 at Highbury one December, one of five league victories in a row, which helped hoist us to the top of the table over Christmas. I was so, so proud.

I was abundantly aware of the importance of our parochial skirmishes against Sunderland and what they meant to the public, something that not all of my predecessors appreciated. But coming from Durham and a village where affiliations were divided, I have a lot of respect for Sunderland. I have nephews who are red and whites, so it's a healthy rivalry, not sinister or violent or nasty. I was delighted when the 2007–08 season ended and Newcastle, Sunderland and Middlesbrough had all avoided relegation, which had appeared a dubious proposition in the preceding months.

I went to all three of Newcastle's triumphant FA Cup finals in the 1950s and revelled in the rich pleasure of victory. Those were joyous moments, but there have been some lean, almost emaciated spells. A dollop of pain nestles among the happier recollections. Pinning your hopes on a team and investing your dreams in their fortunes is not a trivial matter. Newcastle claimed the Inter-Cities Fairs Cup in 1969, but the trophy trail ends there. There have been finals and near misses, but after being such a friend to the club, Wembley's allegiances shifted dramatically, and while Kevin Keegan's side brought thrills and fantasy back to St James', there was something familiar about the agony that accompanied their narrow, exquisite failure to win the title. In 1978, when I won the FA Cup with Ipswich – a minor club in comparison – Newcastle, that weary giant, were relegated, and that hurt me profoundly. I simply didn't understand how it could have happened. In the 1980s, a generation of locally reared talent emerged, including Peter Beardsley, Chris Waddle and Paul Gascoigne, but when Kevin was named manager for the first time in 1992, the club was threatened with extinction. The first task he undertook was to fumigate the training ground.

Kevin set a soaring standard. The football was beautiful, quick and breathless, the club's outlook and wellbeing were transformed beyond measure and the city was gripped by it. What heady days those were, magical days when Newcastle felt young again, transfer records were left in smithereens and nothing seemed impossible. As they rode a wave of euphoria, the growth of the first-team outstripped just about everything else, but Kevin left behind an institution that had finally been restored to its former prominence.

In the intervening years, other managers, most with an elevated profile, have struggled at Newcastle, but I certainly do not regard it as some sort of poisoned chalice. It really should work. It has been a buying club, chairmen have attempted to find money for their managers, they have a fantastic public and a full ground. It is my opinion that only Manchester United and Arsenal have bigger names and stadiums. Newcastle may not have Chelsea's finances, but we're a bigger club. It's all there for a manager to be successful, provided he makes sensible buys, knows the game well, is tactically adept and can motivate players and enforce discipline. But relationships are vital. The manager and his directors are crucial to each other. If it's a good partnership and they're backing each other up, if the scouting network is solid and the purchase of players is sensible and correct, there's no reason why Newcastle can't be in the top five or six every season. The fact that they haven't got that far tells its own story. Managers are not magicians and we need proper tools to do our jobs, not wands. The most crucial aspect, as it always has been, is being given time on the grass.

There has been so much change. Players, staff and regimes have come and gone and fortunes have fluctuated. The one constant in the Newcastle firmament has been the hordes kitted out in black and white. Since the ground was expanded, attendances have rarely slipped much below its capacity of 52,000, which, given the circumstances, is an amazing demonstration of long-suffering loyalty. What is a club in any case? Not the buildings or the directors or the people who are paid to represent it. It's not the television contracts, get-out clauses, marketing departments or executive boxes. It's the noise, the passion, the feeling of belonging, the pride in your city. It's a small boy clambering up stadium steps for the very first time, gripping his father's hand, gawping at that hallowed stretch of turf beneath him and, without being able to do a thing about it, falling in love.

The Messiah returns. Kevin Keegan waves to his adoring public before the league game against Bolton Wanderers on 19 January 2008. After a spell in the doldrums, an entire city was lifted when Kevin strode back through the doors. There was huge happiness and I shared it. The season ended with some good results, although this being Newcastle, uncertainty is seldom far away. A season or two without transition would be enormously beneficial.

8

FURTHER AFIELD

I KNOW that Newcastle features prominently in the title of this book, but I hope it reads like an extended love letter to the whole of the North East. The big city was where my affection for football developed into a searing passion that has stayed with me throughout my life. A circle was squared when I came home to manage the club that once fed my dreams and still pumps through my veins, but I would not be the person I am without the memories and inspiration of my village upbringing in Langley Park. For recreation and other requirements, my family and many others looked south to the Wear as much as north to the Tyne, and given that our community was split between supporters of Newcastle and Sunderland, I've always had respect and affection for the other clubs in the region. It may not be a universal view among fans, but my firm belief has always been that healthy, amicable competition is productive and should be embraced, not feared. Having three teams in the Premier League is of huge benefit to the profile of the region, even if derby games can result in chewed fingernails, lost bets and torment in the workplace.

Both Middlesbrough and Sunderland, who once offered me their manager's job, have been highly supportive to me personally, whether in the backing they have given to my charitable foundation or the welcome they have offered me at their home matches. Parochial allegiances notwithstanding, there is far more to connect than divide us, aside from simple geography. We're working people, with a heritage of heavy industry and a devotion to football.

It seems so fitting to the area and its recent past that Sunderland's Stadium of Light was built on the site of Monkwearmouth Colliery, the last deep mine in the Co. Durham coalfield to close. To mark that fact, there is a giant Davy Lamp outside the ground. 'Into the Light', a phrase that was apparently once found on a sign near the main elevator in the pit – and one that resonates with my own existence – is now emblazoned across the stadium gates.

Black and white have always been my colours and always will be, but in spite of that unswerving loyalty, I'd happily admit to having much more in common with Sunderland and Middlesbrough folk than with other locations in the country.

The sun sets over the Angel of the North – 2008 marked its tenth anniversary. It took me a while to get used to it, but I love the fact that Antony Gormley's remarkable sculpture stands on former mine workings, reminding people that beneath the light there was once a pitch-black world of an economic and social importance that can never be over-estimated. These days, I live very close to the Angel and see it every day. It makes me think of coming home.

ABOVE: Inside the Baltic arts centre, the finishing touches are being put to Antony Gormley's 'Domain Field', metal sculptures taken from the plaster-casted bodies of 286 people, most of them Geordies. The exhibition was one of many critically acclaimed shows to have taken place there. On the top floor of the Baltic, there is a restaurant, where I've taken my wife. Elsie tells me that the ladies' lavatory has walls made from solid glass, offering a sensational, if head-spinning panorama.

LEFT: The graceful span of the Gateshead Millennium Bridge leads your gaze across to the Baltic arts centre. Newcastle's near neighbour across the Tyne cannot be dismissed as a junior partner. Gateshead has been at the forefront of Tyneside's transformation into a heavyweight location for culture and the arts.

PREVIOUS SPREAD: I've had some of the best nights of my life at the Sage Music Centre. Constructed from glass and steel, the £70 million building, which opened in 2004, is a visually stunning addition to the quayside. Through the curved windows, the view across the river to Newcastle is sublime.

The Sage is as impressive inside as it looks from the outside. From rock and pop to classical, jazz and easy listening, just about every musical taste is catered for. The acoustics are superb. There are two auditoriums, one with space for 1,700 seats and the other favouring more intimate concerts. I'd recommend it to anybody.

Swim, ice cream, buy a new record, row – that would have been a dream day, although I'm not convinced that I ever had the money to complete the full set in one fell swoop. Strolling along the riverbank is always a pleasure, while the cathedral and castle above are awe-inspiring. Elsie qualified as a teacher and did her thesis on the cathedral, which is a jaw-dropping sight, from both inside and out.

For a former pitman or anybody with links to colliery life, Durham will always have special connotations. The Durham Miners' Gala, or the Big Meeting, takes place on the second Saturday of every July and I never used to miss it, marching behind the Langley Park colliery banner with my father and brothers to the racecourse to hear the speeches. First, we would walk through our village and everybody would be out, cheering us on. A bus would take us to Durham and we'd parade through the city. I was so proud, a real miner's son. We had a terrific band and a beautiful banner. I was in the scouts and the Church Lads' Brigade, and a member of the colliery band taught me how to play the bugle. I played the 'Last Post' at the cenotaph in Langley Park on Remembrance Sunday as the wreaths were laid. Then we'd go to the tomb of the unknown soldier and do it again. With conflict raging across Europe, it was an emotional time for everybody, and a nerve-wracking task to be asked to perform. I played my little heart out.

Langley Park was my universe back then. I was born in Sacriston, three miles away, but we moved when I was little. I shared a bedroom with my brothers, sleeping top to toe. Elsie lived in Langley Park, too, and we met and courted there, even though I was a professional footballer living in London. We've travelled the world together, but we both feel it's right that we've come back to surroundings where we grew up and met.

To the east of Newcastle lies water. For people of my generation, the coast was where we took our holidays and while our approach to foreign travel has now changed forever, a sunny day still makes us think of the beach and whipped ice cream dribbling down our fingers. Westwards takes you along the A69 to Hexham and Corbridge, across the Pennines and into Cumbria. Roman settlements pepper the route of Hadrian's Wall. This is noble, sweeping, empty countryside. Above us, to the north, a different sort of coastline offers wide, golden beaches, largely unspoilt by human hand, rugged and utterly glorious. Bamburgh Castle, which perches on a steep crag, overlooking sea and village, is imposing and dramatic. Across a causeway, which appears and disappears with the tide, Lindisfarne Priory on Holy Island is important to the history of early Anglo-Saxon Christianity and can be seen from miles around.

RIGHT: The splendour of Durham Cathedral is obvious from the Wear. The riverbank is a smashing spot for a secluded walk and I've had some lovely times there. Once I could swim proficiently, my mother relented and allowed me to go rowing on the river.

OVERLEAF: On alternate Saturdays, when Newcastle weren't playing at home, I'd fill my free time by catching the bus to Durham, where I'd go swimming in the baths or browse for new releases in the record shop. It's a beautiful, picturesque city, and has no haughty airs and graces.

LEFT: Along with the castle, Durham Cathedral has been designated a UNESCO World Heritage Site. Words cannot convey the scale, grace and clout of one of the greatest buildings on the planet – you'll just have to go and visit it. Founded in 1093, it is a monument of Norman splendour, containing the shrine of St Cuthbert and the remains of the Venerable Bede, and has been voted the nation's best-loved building. This view looks towards the east end of the cathedral and the huge Rose Window.

BELOW: Those seeking asylum were once able to claim sanctuary by rapping loudly on the door of the cathedral, using the intricate knocker. The original was cast from bronze and is on display in the Treasury Museum. Criminals would confess their crimes, be given lodgings for thirty-seven days and then be escorted to a port for passage overseas. A modern variant for harassed football managers would be a good idea.

ABOVE: Durham's stained-glass Millennium Window depicts, as well as religious imagery, local scenes, with references to north-east industries and innovations, such as George Stephenson's locomotive engine the Rocket. Among other things, you can see pit workings, glass-blowing, steel and car manufacture, as well as a miner extending the hand of friendship to a bishop.

From Seahouses, boat trips to the Farne Islands, famous for its terns, puffins and seals and the heroism of Grace Darling, can be taken. When I was first immersing myself in football, I remember reading about the Newcastle team being taken to Seahouses for Cup-tie training, a game of golf and a spot of lunch. I can taste the fish and chips now.

Newcastle cannot be looked at in isolation. This is a city that drew coal from the surrounding areas and dispatched it onwards, sending ships on their way to the world. People are still drawn towards it, for its atmosphere, its air of excitement and reputation for innovation. It is still importing and exporting. It is twenty-one miles from Langley Park to Newcastle, which seemed a much greater distance when I was growing up than it does now, when cars are everywhere and journeys are taken in a flash, but the influence of the city spread that far and much farther, too. I would like to think that something is given back in the process. Newcastle is the place it is because of its location, its history, the people who live there, and visit it, but also because of the relationship it has with its surroundings.

LEFT: Having returned to the North East when Newcastle came calling, Elsie and I will never leave. This is a picture of me in 2004, close to our home, back for good in the place I love.

England, the fielding side, take on Zimbabwe at the Riverside Cricket Ground at Chester-le-Street in June 2003. It's a jaw-dropping setting for sport. I'm an honorary member of Durham County Cricket Club and attend matches when I can. I was a decent batsman as a kid. We played in the backstreet with a metal dustbin for a wicket.

Northumberland has some spectacular, spacious scenery – this is looking east from Cockmount Hill towards Cawfields, Hexham. The historic fortifications of Hadrian's Wall run through the region and stretch the entire width of England.

The sun casts a warm glow over the mouth of the Tyne, as viewed from North Shields – natural beauty, industry and heritage roll into one. A lonely tug chugs out to sea. Fishing boats nestle together. The cranes stand idle.

Lobster pots are on display at Seahouses Harbour. A busy fishing port, Seahouses remains a popular tourist spot, offering regular crossings to the Farne Islands and, as you would expect, excellent fish suppers. As a youngster, I remember reading about the Newcastle team heading there for FA Cup training, lunch and a round of golf. Now clubs tend to head for the warmer winter weather of Spain.

9
NEWCASTLE HEROES

MY FATHER used to regale me with stories about Hughie Gallacher, the irascible little Scot with a devil on his shoulder and angels guiding his boots, who approached life with the same ferocity as he played the game. Even in the 1920s, Hughie was a superstar, albeit a troubled one, scoring 133 goals in 160 league appearances for Newcastle, an extraordinary statistic that pales only in comparison to his overall record – 624 senior games, 463 goals. Dad saw him torment defenders, backchat referees, win games single-handed and earn himself an avid following. The idolatry of the famous Number 9 shirt came later – numbering did not become compulsory until the eve of the Second World War – but Gallacher's show-manship and genius mark him out for a special slot in Tyneside folklore.

By the time I embarked on my first wide-eyed trek to St James' Park, when war-time football was being played, Hughie's feats were a matter of memory, but the generation he inspired was now in the team. Albert Stubbins, another destructive striker, was the first player to plant himself in my affections. Full in stature, he was good in the air, sharp and a Newcastle fan, even though he had spent much of his childhood out of the country. He gave me such pleasure and I was beside myself when my father told me he had been sold to Liverpool.

Much later on in life, when I was managing Ipswich, my secretary rang through to tell me she had a Mr Stubbins on the line, a reporter who wanted to speak to me for a moment about a forthcoming match. I took the call. 'Before you say anything, you're not Albert Stubbins by any chance, are you? *The* Albert Stubbins? Albert Stubbins who used to play for Newcastle?' He said he was. I was astounded. It was my bloody hero, ringing me! I felt like a kid again. I was so pleased, so thrilled to speak to him. I told him he could ring me every Friday for the rest of his life and anything he wanted, any story, I'd give him! He was too polite for that, a real gentleman, but we had a few engaging chats. Lovely.

As for so many other people, Jackie Milburn was my next hero. I saw quite a bit of him before I left Langley Park. He played at outside right or striker. We called him Jet because he was so quick – Jackie Jet, taken from the initials of his first names, John Edward Thompson. He was so fast he could catch pigeons.

My first hero and my first heartbreak. Albert Stubbins was the Alan Shearer of his day, a fine header of the ball and a superlative goalscorer. When Newcastle sold him to Liverpool, I felt betrayed but, distraught as I was, I quickly learned that players and managers come and go. It was such a thrill when, decades later, I got to know Albert.

9
NEWCASTLE HEROES

MY FATHER used to regale me with stories about Hughie Gallacher, the irascible little Scot with a devil on his shoulder and angels guiding his boots, who approached life with the same ferocity as he played the game. Even in the 1920s, Hughie was a superstar, albeit a troubled one, scoring 133 goals in 160 league appearances for Newcastle, an extraordinary statistic that pales only in comparison to his overall record – 624 senior games, 463 goals. Dad saw him torment defenders, backchat referees, win games single-handed and earn himself an avid following. The idolatry of the famous Number 9 shirt came later – numbering did not become compulsory until the eve of the Second World War – but Gallacher's showmanship and genius mark him out for a special slot in Tyneside folklore.

By the time I embarked on my first wide-eyed trek to St James' Park, when war-time football was being played, Hughie's feats were a matter of memory, but the generation he inspired was now in the team. Albert Stubbins, another destructive striker, was the first player to plant himself in my affections. Full in stature, he was good in the air, sharp and a Newcastle fan, even though he had spent much of his childhood out of the country. He gave me such pleasure and I was beside myself when my father told me he had been sold to Liverpool.

Much later on in life, when I was managing Ipswich, my secretary rang through to tell me she had a Mr Stubbins on the line, a reporter who wanted to speak to me for a moment about a forthcoming match. I took the call. 'Before you say anything, you're not Albert Stubbins by any chance, are you? *The* Albert Stubbins? Albert Stubbins who used to play for Newcastle?' He said he was. I was astounded. It was my bloody hero, ringing me! I felt like a kid again. I was so pleased, so thrilled to speak to him. I told him he could ring me every Friday for the rest of his life and anything he wanted, any story, I'd give him! He was too polite for that, a real gentleman, but we had a few engaging chats. Lovely.

As for so many other people, Jackie Milburn was my next hero. I saw quite a bit of him before I left Langley Park. He played at outside right or striker. We called him Jet because he was so quick – Jackie Jet, taken from the initials of his first names, John Edward Thompson. He was so fast he could catch pigeons.

My first hero and my first heartbreak. Albert Stubbins was the Alan Shearer of his day, a fine header of the ball and a superlative goalscorer. When Newcastle sold him to Liverpool, I felt betrayed but, distraught as I was, I quickly learned that players and managers come and go. It was such a thrill when, decades later, I got to know Albert.

RIGHT: The Newcastle United team of 1952 was crammed with my idols, including Jackie Milburn, with the ball between his boots. Look at the size of Ronnie Simpson, the goalkeeper. He was tiny in comparison to the giants alongside him, but he compensated for his lack of inches with blink-of-an-eye reflexes and feline agility. No wonder those chiselled faces look so confident. Newcastle had lifted the FA Cup for two years running.

LEFT: Hughie Gallacher, the tough, back-chatting little Scot, who scored goals for fun and left havoc in his wake, was my dad's great favourite. His influence fell heavily on the next generation of Newcastle players, whom I grew up watching. Newcastle has a well-merited reputation for explosive strikers and Hughie is up there with the best of them, but he was a controversial figure who came to a sad end. My brother Tom came across him in ignominious circumstances when he was reduced to sweeping factory floors.

RIGHT: George Robledo (*left*) and Jackie Milburn. George had thighs like tree trunks. He and his brother Ted were from Chile, but in the cold of January 1950, he looks much less chilly than Jackie. What an attacking pair they were. Without badges, the names of kit sponsors or advertising, those long-sleeved shirts look so clean and pure.

Jackie wasn't a Stubbins or a Shearer when it came to aerial prowess, but he was mustard downstairs and he could use space and outpace people. He was a good finisher, too, as well as being an unselfish team-mate.

After I moved to Fulham to begin my own career, Newcastle stayed close to my heart and I saw Jackie grace Wembley in 1951, 1952 and 1955, in a decade that cemented the club's love affair with the FA Cup. Against Blackpool in 1951, Stanley Matthews was expected to be the pivotal performer, but it was Jackie who ran riot, scoring both goals in a 2–0 victory. For the first, he beat the offside trap and whizzed through the middle from the halfway line. The second was an unstoppable shot that Stanley described as the greatest goal he had ever seen.

One legend after another. With his total of 153 goals, Len White is the third most productive striker in Newcastle's history after Jackie and Alan Shearer, and probably the best never to win full international recognition. Len played with Jackie before stepping out of his long shadow to take a more prominent role and make the Number 9 position his own.

Bobby Moncur (*right*) stretches for the ball. Bobby was a respected captain and consistent centre half, both for Newcastle and Scotland. Remembered chiefly for skippering the club to their last major trophy – he scored three goals over the two-legged final – I'm sure Bobby feels ready for that record to be passed on to another man. It's about time.

I actually played against Jackie in a memorable fourth-round Cup-tie with Newcastle at Craven Cottage in January 1956. Fulham trailed 3–0, but we hauled our way back to a 4–3 lead and somehow lost 5–4. That must have been the only time I cursed one of Jackie's goals, but what a game it was. He was another figure whose path would subsequently cross mine. When I became England manager, the Football League had a sponsorship arrangement with Robinson's Barley Water, which involved me naming my young player of the month and, every May, my young player of the year. Across the country, Robinson's hired some illustrious football people to watch games and help me out and they'd send in their recommendations to me. Jackie, one of my original heroes, was my north-east scout, which

took a bit of getting used to, I can tell you. When I used to watch him, I never thought I'd touch him, speak to him or get near him. I'd have fainted. He was a delightful person and his wife was the same.

I had many other favourites during those early halcyon Saturdays. When wingers were first coming to the fore, Bobby Mitchell had a feint and double feint, a paintbrush of a left foot and a lovely, lazy, confident roll on the ball. You never knew which way he was going to go. Frank Brennan was a huge guy, similar in many ways to Jack Charlton, long-legged and tough, who tackled and headed with the best of them. I remember little Ernie Taylor, a tiny but effective distributor of the ball, who could wriggle free of danger. The two Bobbys at full back, Cowell and Corbett, Tom Swinburne in goal, Charlie Crowe, Joe Harvey, Tommy Walker, George Hair, George Robledo and Wor Jackie – they meant so much to me. I was besotted with football and besotted with Newcastle. After most of our visits, we'd run from the match to catch the bus home, but sometimes we'd hang around until the players came out. I'd be there in the throng, a little kid holding out a pencil for a snatched signature. I couldn't contain my enthusiasm. Those men might have come from the moon, they were so exotic and exciting to me. They were like kings, like gods, and because I felt like that, I've always appreciated the sway that football has on young minds, which is why I've very rarely refused an autograph. If there's a queue, I'll see it through, because I remember what that hope and adoration were like.

As my career took off and progressed, I had to focus attention on nurturing my own talent, first as a player and then in the dug-out. Through my father, I kept in touch with the players who were making the Tyneside public purr or growl. Len White assumed Wor Jackie's mantle as Number 9 supreme. I was delighted when, in 1969, Newcastle were led to the Inter-Cities Fairs Cup by Bobby Moncur, the captain, and Wyn Davies, the mighty Welsh striker. Bobby was a model of consistency, a great centre half who covered and defended, headed, tackled and then brought the ball out and passed it. He was a solid man, too.

There would be no more trophies, but the 1970s brought excitement, glamour and, inevitably, its share of disappointment. The most brash and brilliant performer of the lot was a champagne-swilling, cigar-smoking, goal-scoring machine by the name of Malcolm Macdonald, a new breed of celebrity footballer, Newcastle's first modern megastar and a player I introduced to the professional game when I managed Fulham for a short while. The £1,000 we paid Tonbridge Angels for this cocky full back with a wham of a shot probably marks Malcolm down as my best-ever signing.

I had been alerted to him by Harry Haslem, my scout, and we quickly saw that he had a thunderous strike. If we could get him farther up the field, then wow, he would score goals. So we made him a centre forward. I didn't last very long as Fulham manager, but Malcolm had great potential. He was strong with a great physique, muscular, big-shouldered, big thighs, big calves and a very confident boy, even as a kid – not swell-headed or arrogant, but sure of himself, which sometimes is an asset. He had this enormous raw power and could head the ball, too. The trick was to get him on the half-turn, so he was facing the opposition's goalkeeper not his own, and then he'd let fly. He'd hammer the ball when most people would settle for kicking it. After I left, he was sold to Luton Town, then Newcastle, where his swagger and skill and blockbusting goals swiftly endeared him to supporters.

I came across Malcolm again in the 1978 FA Cup final, when my Ipswich side, the upstart underdogs, were up against Arsenal. Malcolm, typically, had been making all sorts of statements in the press, telling everyone what he was going to do to us, how we didn't have a chance. Looking back at their team – Malcolm, Pat Jennings, Pat Rice, David O'Leary, Liam Brady, Frank Stapleton, Alan Hudson – I understood why he said it, although we weren't bad either. I used those comments to stir up Allan Hunter, my tough Northern Ireland centre half. When Arsenal hit their first positive ball into space for Macdonald to spin on to, Allan, who was marking him, came across and whack! He hoofed the ball, Malcolm, the grass and the fresh air into Row Z and if the referee had been in the way, he'd have put him there, too. Malcolm never got a kick and Ipswich won. But he was a great player, a great goalscorer and a genuine legend in black and white.

Sometimes it takes a special figure to lift a club, and Kevin Keegan was certainly that. Everyone knew him when he joined Newcastle – a human dynamo who'd illuminated Liverpool and Hamburg, where he twice won the European Footballer of the Year award – but he struck a chord. The team was quite moribund at the time, stagnating in the old Second Division, but Kevin inspired them. Whether it was his north-east mining heritage, or simply his courage and effervescence, he developed a rapport with supporters that lingers still. Spirited and bubbly, he chased every ball, urging Newcastle to promotion in 1984. After a friendly against Liverpool, in which he bade his farewells, he literally left on a high, with a helicopter touching down on the pitch to whisk him away. A helicopter! When I was sacked by Freddy Shepherd, I left the training ground clutching the golf putter I kept in my office. Some difference!

LEFT: Watched by his team-mate Bobby Moncur, Wyn Davies soars above an Arsenal backline of George Graham and Terry Neil. Wyn wasn't just a great proponent of heading the ball, he was an artist in the air, a bounding Picasso. His moniker 'The Leap' was well merited.

RIGHT: Brash, hard-living and cocky, Malcolm Macdonald can probably be regarded as Newcastle's first modern superstar. His public image could hardly have contrasted more strongly with that of Wor Jackie. I brought Malcolm into the professional game during my brief spell as Fulham manager. He was a full back when we bought him, but his left foot was a bazooka and I was determined to get him closer to goal.

I was abused and spat at by my fellow Newcastle fans when I left Kevin Keegan out of my England squad to face Denmark in 1982. I wanted to try something different, but I never meant such an important player to enter international retirement. I know that Kevin felt hard done by and we both suffered in the aftermath, but my admiration for him was and remains unbroken and our differences are now deep in the past. He electrified my boyhood team when he joined them from Southampton. He did the same again – and much more besides – in management.

A second coming was followed by a third and each of Kevin's three incarnations at St James' has come at a time when fans were craving reason to believe. He came back as manager in 1992 from nowhere – from the golf course. But what a positive impact he had, which marks him down as a remarkable man, because how he did that, I just don't know. The football was adventurous, entertaining and thrilling. Safety from relegation and then promotion were followed by a roller-coaster tilt for the title, which at one stage took them twelve points clear of Manchester United. He must relive those moments every day of his life. His most recent return, in January 2008, was one I witnessed first-hand and it felt like a return to the old days, in the very best sense. Kevin is such a charismatic figure. He inherited a tough situation and a dispirited camp, but he quickly stopped people staring at their shoes, daring them to dream again, and the season finished with some decent football being played. Fingers crossed that it works out.

Kevin hung up his boots at a time when a thick seam of Geordie talent was being plundered. Chris Waddle and Peter Beardsley were both in the Newcastle team, and Paul Gascoigne, who had served as Kevin's boot-boy, would soon follow. I worked with all three on the international scene. Chris could play on either wing and although his left foot was slightly stronger, I liked to play him on the right for England, allowing him to drift inside and then back out again. I think he posed more of a goal threat there. He was a good dribbler and hard-working, although he would often look as though he was carrying a bag of cement on his back. He had that sort of physique. When we did fitness work at high altitude at Colorado Springs in the United States, all the tests showed that he was one of our fittest players. With his hands on his hips, head bowed and breathing hard, he didn't look it, but he had a great heart and lungs. He was a good lad and intelligent about football.

Chrissy, famously, missed one of England's penalties in our 1990 World Cup semi-final against West Germany. He was one of the first to put his hand up and offer to take one. 'No problem,' he said. I'd been in the job for eight years and knew the players very well. I had my own ideas about who should be entrusted with the responsibility, but I threw it open to the group and the individuals who responded were the ones I'd anticipated – Gary Lineker, Peter Beardsley, David Platt, Stuart Pearce, Chris Waddle. I was amazed when Stuart missed – he was our most proficient penalty-taker. I was still quite confident with Chris, though, because he would take them in training like shelling peas, but he did something I'd never seen him do before, leaning back on the shot, going for the high one and putting it miles over the bar. The ball went into orbit. There isn't much consolation to be given in those moments. All of us were rigid with shock. Stuart and Chrissy were disconsolate. Weeping. Stuart, in particular, was a rugged character, but tears were trickling down both of their faces. They were crestfallen, in a bad way emotionally and psychologically. I went up to them and told them they'd done their best and given everything they'd got. 'You can't do any more than that,' I said. 'Forget about it. We've done brilliantly to get here. You'll see. We'll all be heroes when we get home.' There wasn't a lot more I could say. I was in a worse state than both of them.

Peter was a little maestro, pure and simple. He had two sublime bouts at Newcastle, including a wonderful Indian summer under Kevin, and he was a stalwart for me with England. A tremendous player and a clever footballer, full of verve and energy, he was the ideal, unselfish foil for Lineker. He loved running with the ball at his feet and had a great brain. He was very perceptive. Neither he nor Gary were very tall, so there was no point slinging high balls towards them because they would just be headed out by defenders, but anything low or cut back would be a different matter. And what a joy he was to work with. We'd drive somewhere for a training session and when we arrived in the team bus, my staff would unload our gear, the balls and the nets, the bottles of water and the energy drinks. Peter would walk to the dressing-room with his arms full, helping out, doing his bit. That was Peter all over.

What more can I say about a certain exuberant Geordie who elbowed his way into my England squad for Italia '90? Paul Gascoigne was hyperactive, bags of fun and idiotic. He was always up to tricks and was unreliable in many ways because you never knew where he was going, what he'd do when he got there or even whether he'd come back. But stick a ball at his feet and he was Einstein – most of the time. In his first match for England, I brought him on as a late substitute. The midfield was doing well and I didn't want to disturb it, so I put him out on the right, semi-wide. I knew it wasn't his position, but we were winning. 'Stay there,' I said. 'Give us width when we need it, tuck in to defend, get your tackles in and win possession, but remember that I've put you on to give us some width. Stay on the right.' He told me he understood. Within two minutes of setting foot on the pitch he was playing outside left with Chrissy Waddle. He had moved as far away from where I had told him to play as was humanly possible. I was shouting at him, bawling, in fact. When the game finished, I pulled him to one side. 'Paul, I told you what to do. Keep to the right,

I said. What the hell were you playing at?' And do you know what he said to me? 'But Chris is me mate and I wanted to play with him.' We were talking about international football! I was apoplectic. 'Bugger your mate,' I said, 'stick to the right or next time I won't put you on.' That was something he had to learn. He wanted the ball so much he would drift way out of position in his anxiety to get it. But with England he became quite a controllable boy in the end, on the pitch at least. He'd be half-crazed in the dressing-room, absolutely manic, and I'd have to tell him to settle down, but as soon as his boots touched the grass something clicked in. He'd be highly focused, because he just lived for that blessed hour-and-a-half. Perhaps it was the one thing in life that Paul could control.

An admission: I could have signed Gazza for Ipswich, but turned him down. He travelled from his native North East to Suffolk for a trial and although I could see he had something, I never thought he'd make it.

Chris Waddle celebrates with Peter Beardsley in 1984. Two of the most able Geordies to have pulled on boots, they went on to become stalwarts of my England squads, earning well over a hundred caps between them. The North East's reputation for unearthing talent is well deserved, but recognising it and keeping hold of it has been the problem. We must do better.

Peter had a lovely renaissance under Kevin at Newcastle, returning to his first love after productive stints with Liverpool and Everton. A generous, unselfish player, he was a scorer of great goals as much as a great goalscorer, and formed a dazzling fleet-footed partnership with Andy Cole.

LEFT: Wednesday night fever. Paul and Lothar Matthaus adopting similar disco-esque poses as they compete for the ball in that famous World Cup semi-final in 1990. It was his first international tournament, but you could hardly say that England's Geordie midfielder looked out of place in such exalted company. He was brilliant. In terms of consistency, I still think Paul enjoyed his best spell of football under me in Italy.

LEFT: After turning down the chance to sign Paul Gascoigne on schoolboy forms when I was still managing Ipswich – clever on the ball, but too fat, too slow, I thought – I came to realise my mistake. Reports of a chubby, red-faced lad with a fondness for Mars Bars and supreme ability soon filtered down from Newcastle. What a player he was, what a legend he could have been. No respecter of reputations, here Gazza leaves Liverpool's Jan Molby sprawling on the turf. Could he not have found a tighter pair of shorts?

ABOVE: We lost to West Germany on penalties, of course, but Gascoigne's tears became the defining image of England's World Cup campaign. A nation wept with him. For all his attention-hogging antics, Paul wasn't equipped emotionally to deal with the hype of Gazzamania, which we found in full swing on our return. He was such an innocent. We all felt dreadful in that frozen moment, but even though my own international career was coming to an end, it's the manager's job to lift his players. 'You've had a marvellous tournament, son,' I said. 'Look after yourself and keep working hard and there'll be plenty of others.' Sadly not.

Shay Given makes a spectacular save from Manchester United's David Beckham in 2000. A rigorous trainer and an upright man, the Ireland international ranks alongside any of the great goalkeepers I have worked with. Shay has been a superb servant to Newcastle over the years. I'm glad my worst fears weren't realised, but in my time as manager I was always half-expecting Sir Alex Ferguson to pick up the phone and make me an offer. It's a mystery, but no call ever came.

modest celebration. There were never histrionics, just the workmanlike brilliance of a complete centre forward, record goalscorer and a leader. Alan wouldn't know how to be scared, never mind feel it.

For a long while, I admired him from afar. When Alan was at Blackburn Rovers and I was at Barcelona, I tried to sign him, but Ray Harford, the manager, told me he wasn't for sale. He asked politely that we didn't let the Spanish media know of our interest, because the last thing he wanted was

Alan Shearer was far more than just a complete player. He was a leader of men, a Number 9 supreme and a figure of stature. I tried to sign him for Barcelona before I got the chance to watch him at close hand with Newcastle, but he was worth waiting for. He was terrific for me and a joy to work with, vocal in the dressing-room, the perfect professional and a solid role model. I could wish I'd got him with fewer years in his legs, but better late than never would be a massive understatement.

for Alan to become unsettled. I gave Ray my word, kept the promise and a few weeks later he went to Newcastle! Barcelona signed Ronaldo instead, so I didn't fare too badly, and my loss would become my gain when I tipped up at St James' Park. Alan had everything a manager would want. If you had five Shearers in your team, you wouldn't lose a game.

My only twinge of regret – and it's only a twinge – is that I worked with Alan towards the end of his career rather than the start. He was out of the team and struggling when I arrived at Newcastle. Ruud Gullit obviously thought Alan was over the hill. It was a baffling conclusion and a bad miscalculation. Alan had suffered injuries in the past, but he was only twenty-nine and I could see he still had an able body. He'd just gone static. He'd forgotten about working the channels and was standing still waiting for the ball to find him. He responded brilliantly to my encouragement and in my five years at the helm, he did wonderfully well for us. I liked him very much. Great attitude, great on the pitch, he was the kind of character who could win games simply through the force of his own personality.

Saving points is more Shay Given's line of work, and of all the goalkeepers I've worked with at club level – Ipswich, Barcelona, you name it – he is as good as any of them. I'd rate Peter Shilton as the best, but that was with England. Shay is top. I was aware of him before I got to Newcastle, but you can never really say you know somebody until you've looked them in the eyes or stood side-by-side with them, shoulder-to-shoulder in the dressing-room and during matchplay. Shay was a true pro and a great trainer, very likeable, industrious and eager to learn. He had quicksilver reflexes, allowing him to save shots that other keepers wouldn't have reached. When I first started working with him, he wasn't the most astute kicker of a ball. He had Charlie Chaplin feet. Some of his kicking would be as wild as my golf shots, but he worked at it assiduously, practising with his left foot, then his right, and that little imperfection was dealt with through sweat and endeavour. People say he's small for his position, but I don't agree. When you stand next to him, he's a big lad. He had everything in his locker and he didn't have a weak side. He could dive with equal freedom to both his left and his right.

In retrospect, one of the great mysteries is that during all my time on Gallowgate, I never received a single enquiry about him from other clubs. No one ever rang me up and asked, 'Will you sell me your goalkeeper?' I don't know why. During that period I got to know Sir Alex Ferguson very well and I often wondered why Manchester United never came in for Shay. I'm very glad they didn't, but Alex seemed to have problems with his

Michael Owen receives a full-blooded Geordie welcome. Newcastle may not have won trophies in recent years, but when they spent £16 million to bring the England striker home from Real Madrid in 2005, they proved their lingering ability to make trophy signings. Michael has represented more successful teams, but none with more fanatical or loyal support. He's an ice-cool character, but I think even he was taken aback by the size of the crowd who turned up for his unveiling. Unfortunately, injuries have played havoc with his spell in black and white.

keepers and Shay was not only reliable, he was agile and he was brave, diving at the feet of strikers or bursting through a thicket of players to punch or catch. Newcastle can't have been blessed with many better.

So those are the United legends I either watched adoringly or came to know first-hand. It can't be anything other than a personal and incomplete list, because after my early days, scrambling through the turnstiles at St James' Park and tearing towards the unreserved seating, I was away from home for almost half a century. And what makes a hero in any case? It can be a hatful of goals or unstinting loyalty, but it can also be a single moment, a tackle or a dribble, that lodges in the memory and makes a star in stripes. Sometimes it can be potential, brutally curtailed. Geordie friends speak with wistful nostalgia about Tony Green, for instance, even though injury slammed the door on a shimmering future and cruelly restricted him to thirty-five appearances in Newcastle colours.

Michael Owen had represented England, Liverpool and Real Madrid by the time he completed a club-record transfer to Newcastle in 2005. He's a shrewd little cookie, but even so, the day he was unveiled on Tyneside must go down as one of the most amazing of his life. The Toon Army had dispatched a division to greet him. Newcastle were obviously desperate to attract a big player, a household name, one that everybody was familiar with and would get excited about. They paid a lot of money for him, certainly enough to dump Liverpool on their backsides. The reception he received was spectacular. An enormous number of people welcomed him at the stadium and all of us assumed the club had bought a five-star player. Quick, a great little finisher, an individual within the team framework and an unblemished character – hero status appeared guaranteed, but Michael was soon catapulted towards sadness.

Aside from the hamstring tears that are an occupational hazard for little pacy players, his injury record wasn't bad, but his time with us has been very different. With his fractured metatarsal, knee ligament trouble and related ailments, his move to Newcastle hasn't developed in the way he would have liked, and it has taken him time to settle in and produce his dash. I don't know whether the change of manager did the trick, but I do know that Kevin was very supportive of him, helping him regain his confidence and encouraging him to feel that Newcastle was a big club and that by giving his all he could be a success here. The 2007–08 season came to a close with a glimpse of the Michael Owen the country was in thrall to as a youngster, albeit playing in a different position. The captaincy suited him. Better late than never, he looked like a hero again.

A change of manager, his appointment as skipper and a return to full fitness brought out something like the best in Michael. Players love working with Kevin Keegan and it's not difficult to see why. He's a real Mr Motivator, a player's manager. Kevin's decision to play Michael in a more withdrawn role was not something I would have gone with, but it worked well, allowing Newcastle to field two more strikers ahead of him and resulting in goals. Kevin has said Michael can still become a legend at the club. That's something we'd all like to see.

EPILOGUE

IF THE NORTH EAST made me, then the life I've lived in football has certainly shaped the character I was given. It's the nature of the beast that you have to deal with disappointment, but that's what it is – it's not adversity or disaster. Losing matches in such a highly competitive, demanding environment hurts like hell, but you learn that seven days later you'll have another game, another opportunity to win, to put smiles on people's faces and to revel in that fleeting sensation of pleasure and then to do it all again. Managers become men of steel, because you develop the ability to take a hit, get back up and fight again. If a boxer gets knocked down in the ring, he can either stay on the ground or get up and throw the next punch. Whatever faces you, face it. Come out swinging. To survive, you have to do that. And when it comes to football, I've endured.

That process of getting over defeat, responding to sadness or recovering from a blow has helped me in my grimmer moments. I've had a great life, I really have. When I look back on everything I've done and seen, the experiences I've had, the myriad colours and memories, I don't feel as though I've ever been ill. I'll puff out my chest and say to Elsie, 'I've been fit all my life, I have.' She'll look at me as if I'm daft. 'Bobby, what are you talking about? You've had cancer five times.' She's right of course, but it rarely interrupted my work and never detracted from my enjoyment of living. If you're 2–0 down at half-time, what do you do? You look at where the game is going wrong and why, what you're going to do about it, what you'll change or which player you'll replace. Deal with the problem and you've got a chance. If you don't, it will only get worse.

I've always been a fighter. Without that quality, you won't get very far. After first being diagnosed with cancer during my spell at PSV Eindhoven, I went to FC Porto, when it happened again, far more seriously. This time it was a malignant melanoma in my face. I needed an operation to take my teeth out, cut through the roof of my mouth and make sure everything was removed. Afterwards, I required radiotherapy and, for the rest of my days,

Elsie and I have a wonderful life together. Adapting to my illness and disability has been a test, but I will not give in to it. I've never shirked a challenge and have no intention of starting now.

attention, the media response was good and we were up and running. I've thrown myself into it, as I have with everything, like moving to Barcelona and learning a new language. I've always loved work. There have been occasions when I've taken Ruth to one side and said, 'What have you bloody well got me into?' and there have been times when I haven't been too well, but I've not missed a single meeting. The original intention was that I wasn't going to do much, that I would be a figurehead and float about in the background, but it hasn't worked out like that. I've put my back into it. If I'm committed to something, then I'm committed.

My original concern was groundless. Within the first seven weeks, the first target had been met and £560,000 had been raised. It has entailed more effort than I ever imagined and Judith has been amazing – we couldn't have managed without her organisational skills. She's been chief fundraiser, chauffeur and banker – but the response has been humbling, heart-rending and uplifting. Our very first donation set the trend. Soon after the formation of the charity was announced, Elsie and I had a visitor to our home. The lady on our doorstep was clutching an envelope full of cash. She told us that her husband had died recently and his final request was that instead of mourners buying flowers for his funeral, he wanted a collection to be held for my charity. So there she was, carrying out his wish. She handed over £271.74. What can you say to that?

Johnny Bliss is a singer, a member of the Showman's Guild and a local lad. He typifies the people up here. He read about the Foundation and, without getting in touch, decided to raise some money for me. He held a concert and sold some CDs. So far, so selfless. But Johnny has pancreatic cancer. He had been told by his doctors that he had months to live. He didn't have much time left, but he was thinking about others. His story just hit me for six. I met him in the Copthorne. He brought his whole family, made the men wear their best suits and ties. All told, they had raised about £10,000. You could see he wasn't well. I could have cried.

On the website we set up to accept donations, people have left some incredibly moving comments – 'Keep going, Bobby', 'You need the money? Enough said, you've got it.' So much has come from small donors, people for whom five pounds or a tenner really means something. People have stopped me in the street to hand me notes. I went to watch Sunderland play Middlesbrough towards the end of the 2007–08 season. I was in the back row of the directors' box, which saves me from having to go up and down steps, and at the end of the game I stood up to leave. 'Hey, hey, Bobby!' shouted two voices in unison. It was a pair of old chaps in the next section.

Part of my latest team. It's an experienced line-up, but with plenty of quality. I'm pictured here with oncologist Dr Ruth Plummer, who set the ball rolling for The Sir Bobby Robson Foundation when she asked if I knew anybody who could help fund a new cancer trials facility at Newcastle's Freeman Hospital. The response has been incredible. My friends Jim Rosenthal, Bob Wilson and Des Lynam kindly attended our launch at the Copthorne Hotel. I've always loved a challenge, always relished hard work and I've thrown myself into the task of raising money. This time it's about beating death, not another football team. And it's about giving something back to the part of the world that means more to me than any other.

One gave me £20, the other £10. At that moment, there was no thought of north-east rivalry. It's happened to me a lot. By the end of a dinner I held at St James' Park, my pockets were full of notes, cheques and loose change. A woman came up to me with her husband to thank me for what I was doing. She was very tearful, very emotional. He was misty-eyed. She told me that she'd lost her boy, Jordan Thompson, a Newcastle Academy player, a few months earlier at fifteen years of age, and they'd bought a table at my dinner because they wanted to support us. How do you respond to that? If that had happened to me ... well, how would you cope? It's an horrific disease, but I can honestly say that cancer has shown me the best of people, too. I just think that with time and money, we'll conquer it eventually. What I'm doing is a drop in the ocean compared with others – all around the world, endeavour is going into how we combat it and how we might cure it – but I've decided that with whatever time I've got left, I'm going to try to help people fight. I've had a life in football and left a legacy with that, but this is just as important to me.

My own battle goes on. For some reason, I'm the only person in my family who has been struck in this way, so you could say I'm unlucky, but I've been lucky, too – every time the cancer has been found quickly. Early detection means early treatment. A growth was discovered on my lung. I had a biopsy and was told it was malignant but, on the positive side, it was the only tumour in my body. 'So get it out,' I said. Fine, I thought. I didn't realise they were going to take a third of my lung away and that I'd be side-tracked for three months, but I never worried about it. That old football mentality again – bring on the next match and new opposition. I got it, too.

It can come out of the blue. I was the fittest seventy-year-old in the country when I was managing Newcastle; two years later I was grappling with death. I was at a match – where else would I have been on a Saturday at three o'clock? It was at Ipswich, the first game of the season, and I'd just received a thunderous reception from supporters, having been named the club's honorary president. By 3.15 or so, not that I knew much about it, something had happened to me. By 5.30, I had been told I had a tumour on the brain. Hours earlier, I'd felt like Tarzan – I could have swung from the trees if I'd wanted to. I was able to run, I was fit and strong. Even then, I thought I'd be in hospital for a couple of days, no more. The day before I went in to have the tumour removed, I was on the roof of my house with my son, Mark, clearing the leaves. I planned to cut the grass when I got back.

When I woke up paralysed after my brain operation, I knew I was in for the long haul. Four days later, I couldn't walk or stand up. I was convinced

I'd be in a wheelchair for the rest of my life. My arm was swollen – it looked like I'd hit a wall with it – so the nurses used to put it in a sling to let it drain. I felt tired, so I rang the bell. I could feel myself sliding away. Apparently, I'd collapsed and had a blackout, but they thought I'd suffered a heart attack. When I came around after about twenty minutes, all these people were around my bed. I was taken downstairs for a scan and they found a blood clot next to my heart. If it had travelled two inches more, I'd have been finished. I'd had an aneurism. The professor who did the operation came in to see me and told me I was lucky to be alive.

'You actually should be dead,' he said.

'But I'm not,' I replied.

'No, you're not. But you should be. What's happened to you is remarkable and we can't believe you're alive. Most people wouldn't have got over it.' My strong heart and active lifestyle had probably saved me. I had another aneurism after I got out.

The disability I suffered as a result of the operation is my biggest frustration, not the cancer itself. If I could play golf, drive my car, do the gardening or even tie my tie or my own shoelaces, I'd feel a lot better. The fact that I'm completely dependent on Elsie, my family, or Judith to get out of the house or go anywhere has been difficult to come to terms with. I'm not bitter about it, but I never thought I'd finish like this. I guess nobody does. I thought I would live until I was eighty-six and then go suddenly, like my dad. But I try to deal with it. I've got an exercise bike and although I get tired, I do my repetitions. I've got a plan. I also have some amazing people to take care of me.

After my lung operation, I had to keep having check-ups, to make sure that nothing new had materialised. One scan was to bring some devastating news. Tumours in my lungs again. Malignant again. I went to see Professor Kelly at Newcastle General to discuss these latest findings. Elsie couldn't come with me, because she happened to be poorly that day. Dr Kelly told me this time the tumours weren't operable. I realised he was telling me that I had a bleak future. So I said, 'Right, how long have I got?'

'Well, nobody knows,' Dr Kelly replied. 'Not weeks, of course, but not years either. Months.'

'How many months?'

'I don't know. Maybe eight. Maybe twelve. Maybe more. We don't know.'

Bloody hell, I thought. Bloody hell. It was a shock, I can tell you. I had a fight for life on my hands. When the doctor said not weeks, not years, but months, he stopped me in my tracks.